Data Protection:

Legal Compliance and Good Practice for Employers

Data Protection:

Legal Compliance and Good Practice for Employers

Second edition

Lynda A C Macdonald

Tottel Publishing
Maxwelton House
41–43 Boltro Road
Haywards Heath
West Sussex
RH16 1BJ

British Library Cataloguing-in-Publication Data

A CIP Catalogue record for this book is available from the British Library.

ISBN 978 1 84766 262 0

Typeset by Kerrypress Ltd, Luton, Beds

Printed and bound in Great Britain by CPI Anthony Rowe Ltd, Chippenham, Wiltshire

About the Author

Lynda Macdonald

Lynda Macdonald is a self-employed freelance employment law trainer, advisor and writer. For fifteen years, prior to setting up her own business, she gained substantial practical experience of employee relations, recruitment and selection, dismissal procedures, employment law and other aspects of human resource management through working in industry. With this solid background in human resource management, she successfully established, and currently runs, her own business in employment law and management training/consultancy. She is also appointed as a panel member of the Employment Tribunal service in Aberdeen, where she lives.

Lynda is a university graduate in language and a Chartered Fellow of the Chartered Institute of Personnel and Development. Additionally, she has an LLM degree in employment law.

Lynda has to date written thirteen books on various aspects of employment law, all of which have been published by well-known national publishers.

Contact Lynda at: lyndamacdonald@clara.co.uk

Web site: www.lyndamacdonald.co.uk

Contents

Contents

Contents

Table of statutes

Table of cases

Chapter 1   Overview of the Data Protection Act 1998

Introduction

1.1   The *Data Protection Act 1998* (*DPA 1998* or 'the Act') aims to protect individuals' personal information, or personal data, as it is known. Those who work in the field of human resources (HR) manage large amounts of often very confidential data, from past criminal convictions to health information, to information about racial origins and so on. The Act sets out the law on how that data can be handled and used. It gives individuals in most cases the right to request access to the data held about them personally by making a 'subject access request'.

The Act requires employers to handle data in accordance with eight data protection principles which are the subject of CHAPTER 2 of this book. Any person or organisation holding personal data is called a 'data controller' and they must notify the Information Commissioner that they hold the data and the purposes for which they hold it. This process of notification is examined in CHAPTER 3.

The Information Commissioner's Office (ICO) is the UK's independent authority set up to promote access to official information and to protect personal information. Its website, www.ico.gov.uk, contains a great deal of useful information for employers and other interested parties. For example, it contains a lengthy guide (105 pages) titled 'Data Protection 1998 – Legal Guidance'. More directly relevant to employers, the Employment Practices Code, which can be freely downloaded from the website, is an extremely useful and relevant document. Its aim is to help employers to comply with the DPA and to encourage them to adopt good practice, striking a balance between the legitimate expectations of workers that personal information about them will be handled properly and the legitimate interests of employers in deciding how best to run their businesses. The Code is divided into four parts which deal with recruitment and selection (part 1), employment records (part 2), monitoring at work (part 3) and information about workers' health (part 4). The Code is referred to extensively in later chapters of this book.

This book aims to provide detailed information and guidance to employers on how to comply with the data protection legislation and ensure good practice throughout every aspect of employment.

Key purposes of data protection legislation

1.2 The *DPA 1998* was brought into force on 1 March 2000 in the UK in order to comply with an EU directive (implemented in 1995) on data protection The aim of the legislation is to ensure that the privacy rights of individuals are respected and that data is processed fairly and lawfully.

In relation to employment, the Act is designed to:

- require employers to comply with eight data protection principles, with a view to protecting all personal information held about individuals;

- require employers to determine how and why they process personal information about their employees and others;

- protect the privacy and other rights of individuals in respect of information held about them by the employer;

- strike a balance between the reasonable needs of employers to keep records about their staff and the rights of employees to have respect for their private life;

- eliminate any collection of personal information that is irrelevant or excessive to the employment relationship; and

- allow individuals to gain access to any information held about them.

History of the Act

1.3 The *DPA 1998* repealed and replaced the *Data Protection Act 1984*. The earlier Act covered only personal data that was held in computerised systems and not manually held data.

When the *DPA 1998* was first implemented, there was a 'transitional relief period' relating to personal data that was held in manual files created before 24 October 1998 (the date the Act should have been implemented). This allowed employers who held employment records a period of grace during which they could continue to process these records under less rigorous conditions than those imposed by the *DPA 1998*. The transitional period lasted nine years, and expired on 23 October 2007.

Any employer that has not already done so would be well advised now to review old manual files, tidy them up and remove any information that is no longer relevant.

The importance of compliance – penalties and risks

1.4 Breach of the Act is a criminal offence. The principal offences are processing without a notification and recording or using personal data unlawfully. Furthermore, *section 55* of the Act makes it an offence (with certain exemptions) to obtain, disclose or procure the disclosure of personal information knowingly or recklessly, without the consent of the organisation holding the information. Offences are punishable by a fine of up to £5,000 in a magistrates' court and an unlimited fine in the Crown Court. Alternatively, a prison sentence can be imposed of up to two years. It is also an offence to process personal data without having first registered (see CHAPTER 3) as a data controller.

Under more recent provisions brought into force by the *Criminal Justice and Immigration Act 2008*, the Information Commissioner has the power to impose a 'monetary penalty notice' (ie a fine) in respect of any serious contravention of the data protection principles which was deliberate and which occurred in circumstances where the employer knew, or ought to have known, that the contravention would occur and that it would be likely to cause substantial damage or distress to one or more individuals.

Additionally, anyone who has suffered damage through a breach of the legislation can sue for damages.

Breach of the Act can also lead to:

- a criminal record;
- requirement to correct a practice which breaches the Act;
- very bad publicity such as 'ABC Bank plc publishes customer bank account details on the internet' or 'Individuals who ordered Viagra find their personal details pasted on the net' etc.

As stated above, individuals can sue for compensation in the event that their rights under the DPA are breached. There are no specific guidelines as to appropriate levels of compensation for a claim under the Act. The judge hearing the case has discretion in these matters and would take many factors into consideration including the seriousness of the breach and the effect upon the claimant. The level of distress caused to the claimant as a result of the breach of the Act would be particularly important.

Audits

1.5

Running through most of the Information Commissioner's guidance is advice that organisations should undertake audits – general audits of their data protection policies and procedures and specific audits such as checking what the effects would be if they were to introduce a particular kind of monitoring.

The aim of an audit is:

- to ensure the rules are not breached in the first place; and

- to show where a breach of the rules has occurred.

The Information Commissioner has published a substantial 166-page audit manual which employers can download from the website. The manual contains a methodology for conducting data protection compliance audits and lots of useful checklists to complete in order to assess whether or not a business is compliant with the main provisions of the *DPA 1998*. Rather than simply being tailored to the Commissioner's specific needs, it has been written in such a way that any employer can use it to help judge their own data protection compliance. The manual is divided into four main parts which deal with the audit method, the audit process, general guidance on auditing and a series of annexes providing essential documents such as checklists containing compliance questions for each of the Act's main features and other pro-forma documents.

Personal liability

1.6 Under the *DPA 1998, section 61*, if a company commits a criminal offence under the Act, any director, manager, secretary or similar officer or someone purporting to act in any such capacity is personally guilty of the offence in addition to the corporate body if the offence:

- was committed with their consent or connivance; or

- is attributable to any neglect on their part.

Where the affairs of a corporate body are managed by its members, any member who exercises the functions of management as if they were a director can also be guilty of the offence that results from any of their acts or omissions.

Government departments are not liable to prosecution under the Act, but individual civil servants may be prosecuted if they personally are believed to be guilty of an offence under the *DPA 1998, section 55* (the unlawful obtaining or disclosure of personal data), or obstructing or failing to assist in the execution of a warrant issued in accordance with the Act (*Schedule 9, para 12*).

Offences include:

- processing without notification (*section 21(1)*);

- failure to notify the Commissioner of changes to the register entry (*section 21(2)*);

- processing before expiry of assessable processing time limits or receipt of assessable processing notice within such time (*section 22(6)*);

- failure to comply with written request for particulars (*section 24*);

- failure to comply with an enforcement notice, or information notice, or special information notice (*section 47(1)*);

- knowingly or recklessly making a false statement in compliance with an information notice or special information notice (*section 47(2)*); and

- intentional obstruction of, or failure to give reasonable assistance in, the execution of a warrant (*Schedule 9*).

Also, under *section 55* it is an offence for a person, knowingly or recklessly, without the consent of the data controller, to:

- obtain or disclose personal data or the information contained in personal data; or

- procure the disclosure to another person of the information contained in personal data.

The Act provides specific exceptions to liability for this offence where the person can show that:

- the obtaining, disclosing or procuring:

  - was necessary to prevent or detect crime; or

  - was required or authorised by law;

- they acted in the reasonable belief that they had the legal right to obtain, disclose or procure the disclosure;

- they acted in the reasonable belief that the data controller would have consented to the obtaining, disclosing or procuring if the data controller had known; or

- in the particular circumstances the obtaining, disclosing or procuring was justified as being in the public interest.

A person will not be guilty of this offence if the personal data in question fall within the national security exemption at *section 28*.

Where employees of a data controller organisation have authority to obtain and disclose personal data in the course of their employment (for example bank employees who can access customer accounts for banking purposes), they will commit these offences if they use their position to obtain, disclose, or procure disclosure of personal data for their own purposes.

Under *section 56*, unless one of the statutory exceptions apply, it is an offence for a person to require another person or a third party to:

- supply him or her with a relevant record (see below); or

- produce a relevant record to him or her;

in connection with:

- the recruitment of that other person as an employee;

- the continued employment of that other person;

- any contract for the provision of services to him or her by that other person; or

- where a person is concerned with providing (for payment or not) goods, facilities or services to the public or a section of the public, as a condition of providing or offering to provide any goods, facilities or services to that other person.

The statutory exceptions to liability for such offences are:

- that the imposition of the requirement was required or authorised by law; or

- that in the particular circumstances the imposition of the requirements was justified as being in the public interest.

The Act provides that the imposition of the requirement is not to be regarded as being justified in the public interest on the ground that it would assist in the prevention or detection of crime.

Enforcement

1.7 The Information Commissioner is in charge of data protection enforcement in the UK. If an employer receives a request for information or formal notice from the Information Commissioner, it should be taken very seriously indeed and ideally legal advice sought on the implications and what should or should not be said or done by way of response.

The Information Commissioner has the power to serve 'information notices' on employers either on his own volition or where there has been a request for an assessment. The notice will tell the employer to provide information to the Information Commissioner and give a time limit by which this must be provided.

The Act also gives the Commissioner powers to serve enforcement notices on employers where there has been a contravention of one of the data protection principles. The notice will specify what the employer must do, such as stop processing data in breach of the Act.

In addition, the Information Commissioner has the power (under the Criminal Justice and Immigration Act 2008) to impose a 'monetary penalty notice' (ie a fine) on an organisation that has acted in serious contravention of the data protection principles in circumstances where the contravention was deliberate and where the employer knew, or ought to have known, that the contravention would occur and that it would be likely to cause substantial damage or distress to one or more individuals.

Inspections

1.8   If there are reasonable grounds for suspecting that an employer is committing or has committed an offence under the Act, or is contravening or has contravened any of the data protection principles, the Information Commissioner may apply to a circuit judge (sheriff in Scotland and county court judge in Northern Ireland) for a warrant to enter and search the employer's premises. Before issuing a warrant, the judge will need to be satisfied that there are reasonable grounds for the Information Commissioner's suspicion and that:

- the Commissioner has already demanded access to the premises by giving seven days' written notice to the occupier; and

- access was demanded at a reasonable hour and was unreasonably refused; or

- although entry to the premises was granted, the employer unreasonably refused to comply with a request by the Information Commissioner's officers to allow any of the necessary procedures to be carried out; and

- the Commissioner has notified the employer of the application for the warrant and that the employer has had an opportunity to be heard by the judge as to whether or not the warrant should be issued.

If, however, the judge is satisfied that the case is urgent or that giving notice to the employer would defeat the object of the entry, the judge may issue the warrant without notice having been given to the occupier.

The warrant will authorise the Information Commissioner or any of his officers or staff to:

- enter and search the specified premises at any time within seven days of the date of the warrant;

- inspect, examine, operate and test any equipment found there which is used or intended to be used for the processing of personal data; and

- inspect and seize any documents or other material found there which may be evidence of an offence or contravention of the *DPA 1998*.

It is a criminal offence:

- intentionally to obstruct a person in the execution of a warrant; or

- to fail, without reasonable excuse, to give anyone executing a warrant such help as may reasonably be required to execute the warrant.

Employers should seek legal advice if notice is given of an inspection visit.

The value of having a data protection policy

1.9 Every employer should devise and implement a data protection policy (although the contents will vary from organisation to organisation). The policy should be communicated to all members of staff and those who deal with personal data as part of their jobs should be thoroughly trained. The policy should also, of course, be reviewed regularly and, when necessary, updated.

Appointing a responsible person

1.10 It is important for all employers to identify who within their organisation will hold overall responsibility for data protection issues, and for ensuring that all the employer's policies, procedures and practices comply with the *DPA 1998* and the general guidelines given in the Employment Practices Code.

The person appointed to hold such responsibility should ideally be a senior manager who has sufficient authority to challenge any practices that might risk being in breach of legislation or associated codes of practice and make decisions about data protection compliance. In a large organisation, a senior HR manager would be an ideal candidate for such responsibility, whilst in a small business it may be appropriate for the owner or managing director to hold responsibility. Alternatively, the company secretary could be the nominated person.

The responsible person should aim to achieve a coordinated approach to the issue of data protection, since the topic demands input and cooperation from people in a range of different posts throughout the organisation. In effect, data protection is a multi-disciplinary matter. The responsible person should therefore take steps to ensure that all line managers receive appropriate training to enable them to understand their responsibilities under data protection legislation.

The responsible person should also be charged with ensuring that all the employer's policies and procedures are regularly checked, in particular against the *DPA 1998* and the Employment Practices Code. The responsible person should also be made accountable for ensuring that policies and procedures are consistently put into practice by all staff, and especially by those whose jobs take them into contact with personal data held about employees. In particular, HR staff, payroll employees, line managers and possibly IT staff may have access to personal information about individuals and the responsibility for ensuring the ongoing training of these individuals in data protection matters will have to be ensured.

Someone who is newly appointed to the role that involves responsibility for data protection issues may wish to review and deal with the following matters:

- whether the organisation has a valid notification in the register of data controllers;

- what personal data about employees (and others) exists within the organisation and where and by whom it is held;

- whether it is necessary or appropriate for individuals other than HR staff to hold personal data about staff;

- the type of information held and whether it is genuinely appropriate and necessary in light of the needs of the organisation;

- whether any information routinely collected about employees or job applicants is irrelevant or excessive when viewed against the employer's legitimate needs and whether the employer should consequently refrain from collecting it (or destroy it);

- whether reliable processes are in place for ensuring the proper destruction of paper and computerised files when they are no longer needed by the organisation;

- where sensitive data is collected, whether one of the conditions for the processing of sensitive data is satisfied (see CHAPTER 4);

- whether those who have access to personal data are aware of their legal responsibilities under the *DPA 1998*, including the fact that they may be held personally liable for any breach of the Act;

- whether clear data protection guidelines have been devised and communicated to all staff who may have access to personal data in the course of performing their jobs;

- whether staff who have access to personal data in the course of their jobs have received proper training in the provisions of the *DPA 1998*;

- whether employees who have access to personal information in the course of their work have signed confidentiality and security clauses;

- whether newly recruited staff are properly informed of the employer's data protection rules and guidelines during induction.

One of the tasks of the senior person in charge of data protection matters might be to select an 'off-the-shelf' computer package to manage the employer's personnel records. In this eventuality, the employer should ensure the computer system they purchase is fully data protection compliant. It will not be open to an employer to 'blame the computer' if their data protection measures fail to conform to the Act, nor to argue that the responsibility for their failure to comply with the Act rests with the supplier of the computer system. The responsibility for compliance with the Act rests plainly with each employer, rather than with any organisation that has supplied them with a computer system or that manages data on their behalf.

When purchasing a computerised personnel records system, the employer may also wish to satisfy themselves that the system will readily enable them to retrieve all the information about any individual employee on receipt of a subject access request.

The Data Protection Forum is an organisation that deals with data protection matters in the UK. Their website (www.dpforum.org.uk) states:

> 'The Data Protection Forum is an association of organisations from all sectors, formed to provide a focus for the exchange, analysis and communication of information on all matters relating to the protection of personal information and compliance with Data Protection law, and more recently compliance with Freedom of Information.'

Employers may find this forum useful.

The role of the HR department

1.11 The *DPA 1998* creates many responsibilities and liabilities for HR managers and practitioners. In most organisations (other than small businesses), it will be the HR department that is expected to manage and control employment records and advise line managers as to the implications of data protection legislation in the context of people management and the recording and use of employee information.

The issue of data protection should of course be viewed not only as an HR responsibility, but rather as an integral part of good general management. The aim should be to mainstream data protection into all the organisation's policies, procedures and practices in order to promote openness and transparency in the collection and use of personal information about employees, whilst at the same time ensuring security of the information held, the protection of confidential information and respect for employees' right to privacy. It will usually fall to HR to strive to achieve a coordinated approach to data protection, since the topic demands input and cooperation from people in a range of different posts throughout the organisation.

This matter should not, however, be left to chance. The employer should allocate clear responsibility for every aspect of data protection to a senior person within the organisation, ideally an HR director or senior HR manager who has sufficient authority to challenge any policies or practices that might risk being in breach of legislation. This senior manager should have sufficient authority to make and enforce decisions about data protection compliance. They should also be charged with ensuring that all the employer's policies and procedures are regularly checked against the Act and the recommendations contained in the Employment Practices Code. An equally important responsibility will be to ensure that policies and procedures are consistently put into practice by all staff, especially by those whose jobs take them into contact with personal data held about employees (or customers, suppliers, etc).

It will be up to HR to make sure that all staff, and in particular line managers, fully understand their responsibilities under the Act and that those whose jobs take them into contact with personal data receive full training in data protection matters. In particular, employees who deal with personal data in the course of their jobs should be made aware that they can personally be held liable for a breach of the Act, for example if they use personal data for an illegitimate purpose or disclose it without the authority to do so. This could be in addition to the employer's liability to pay compensation to any employee who has suffered damage as a result of a breach of the Act.

HR managers will also be responsible in most organisations for handling requests from employees for access to data held about them. It will be important for HR to devise and implement a reliable and efficient system for handling such requests, having previously ensured that all locations where personal information is held are known and that all personal information, whether held manually or on computer, is readily accessible.

Security

1.12 The need for security of all personal information held about an organisation's employees is one of the key features of the *DPA 1998*. Ensuring security of personal information will necessarily involve checking:

- access to buildings, computer rooms and offices where personal information is held;

- access to computer and other equipment where unauthorised access could have a detrimental effect on security;

- that manual records are put away at night in locked filing cabinets before the cleaners arrive;

- that passwords are not written down so that others can access them;

- that strict rules are in force within the business about what personal information can be accessed by which employees, for example the information that line managers can access about their staff should be different to (and less than) that which an HR manager can access;

- that there is an efficient security system in place to prevent employees from seeing other employees' details;

- that mechanisms are in place to detect any breach of security, and procedures in place to investigate such breaches;

- that all staff have undergone training on the organisation's data protection policy and how it works in practice, either as part of their induction or at specialist sessions appropriate for their job function (preferably both).

It is becoming common for employees in certain jobs to perform some or all of their work at home. In many ways, jobs relating to processing and use of personal data are very well adapted to home-working. The employer needs, however, to ensure that there is sufficient security in place. If the employee is working at the kitchen table with friends and family, who may potentially be able to read screens or look at papers, coming in and out all day then home working involving particularly sensitive data may not be permissible. Before agreeing to a home-working arrangement, the employer should (with the employee's consent) check out the employee's home for this purpose. It may be appropriate to require the employee (as a term of their contract) to set aside a room for their work at home. Locks and other security measures should also be checked.

Management of data protection

1.13   The issue of data protection should be viewed as an integral part of good management and should, arguably, be mainstreamed into the employer's policies, procedures and practices. Employers should therefore seek to incorporate data protection principles into all their policies and procedures, including those on recruitment, references, record keeping, discipline, sickness absence, security, computer use and monitoring. In this way issues such as security, confidentiality of information and privacy will become the norm within the workplace and the employer will be in a much stronger position to ensure compliance with the *DPA 1998*.

As the law stands at present, there is no specific duty to consult trade unions or workers' representatives on data protection matters. Despite this absence of a duty to consult, consultation is to be recommended in that it can help the employer to ensure that their data processing practices are fair, transparent and acceptable to their employees, thus increasing trust and respect in employment relationships.

Chapter 2   The data protection principles

Introduction

2.1   The *Data Protection Act 1998* (*DPA 1998*, or 'the Act') requires that businesses holding personal data must follow eight data protection principles. How they apply in the HR area is summarised in the Information Commissioner's Employment Practices Code and examined in more detail in CHAPTER 5 (Part 1 of the code – recruitment and selection), CHAPTER 6 (Part 2 of the Code – employment records), Chapter 7 (health records – Part 2 and also Part 4 of the Code on medical records) and CHAPTER 9 (monitoring – Part 3 of the Code). This chapter examines the eight data protection principles contained in the Act and in particular the obligations which they impose on employers and their staff. The Act imposes general and, in some cases fairly loosely worded, obligations on those handling personal data as to how they obtain and use it. *DPA 1998, section 4(4)* provides that it is the duty of the 'data controller to comply with the data protection principles in relation to all personal data with respect to which he or she is the data controller'. This applies to all employers who process personal data about their employees. The data protection principles themselves are set out in *DPA 1998, Schedule 1*, which also elaborates on what the principles mean. These form the core of the Act.

In summary, the eight data protection principles compel employers to ensure that personal information about individuals is:

1   processed fairly and lawfully;

2   obtained only for one or more specified and lawful purposes, and not processed for any purpose(s) that is incompatible with those stated purposes;

3   adequate, relevant and not excessive in relation to the purpose(s) for which it was obtained;

4   accurate and, where necessary, kept up to date;

5   not kept for longer than is necessary in relation to the purpose(s) for which it was obtained;

6   processed in accordance with individuals' rights under the *DPA 1998*;

7   protected by appropriate technical and organisational measures against unauthorised or unlawful processing, accidental loss or destruction, and damage;

8   not transferred outside the European Economic Area unless the country or territory to which it is transferred has in place an adequate level of protection for individuals' rights and freedoms in relation to the processing of personal data.

The principles are explored more fully at 2.2–2.8 below in the context of their practical application in employment.

The first principle: fair and lawful processing

The duty to process data fairly and lawfully

2.2   The first data protection principle creates the obligation on employers to process personal data 'fairly and lawfully'. This duty is subject to the proviso that personal data must not be processed unless one of a number of conditions is fulfilled. The conditions are that:

●   the employee has given their consent to the processing, ie has signified agreement by some positive means; or

●   data processing is necessary for one of the following reasons:

–   for the performance of a contract, for example the processing of employees' wages;

–   in order to ensure compliance with a legal obligation, for example information about an employee's working hours may be necessary in order to comply with the *Working Time Regulations 1998 (SI 1998 No 1833)*;

–   to protect the vital interests of the employee, for example the disclosure of an employee's medical details to a hospital casualty department on discovering that the employee had been admitted following an accident would be legitimate;

–   for the administration of justice or for the exercise of any public functions (this condition has no general application to employers);

–   for the purposes of legitimate interests pursued by the employer, for example if the business was about to be transferred.

Further conditions are imposed on the processing of data where it is classed as 'sensitive data' under the Act (see 4.6 below).

It is important to note the word 'necessary' used in this part of the Act. If the employee's consent has not been obtained, data about that person can be processed only if one of the relevant conditions is necessary for the business, and not just because (for example) management would find it convenient.

Where data processing is being done in order to comply with a legal obligation, or is done for any purpose authorised by legislation, it will be lawful. An example could be the processing of data obtained as a result of an exercise to monitor employees' use of the organisations' email or telephone system. Provided the monitoring was conducted for one of the purposes authorised by the *Telecommunications (Lawful Business Practice) (Interception of Communications) Regulations 2000*, it would be lawful (see CHAPTER 9 for a full discussion of this topic).

Fairness, however, is quite another matter. It is theoretically possible for data processing to be lawful but unfair. If, for example, the processing of personal data is excessive or carried out without good cause, it could be unfair even though it may not overtly be in breach of any statutory provisions. Similarly the obtaining of personal data through deception might not be against the law, but would almost certainly be unfair. *Schedule 1, Part II* of the *DPA 1998* provides that regard should be paid to the method by which information is obtained, including whether any person from whom it is obtained is deceived or misled as to the purpose(s) for which it is to be processed. Employers should therefore be vigilant to ensure they do not deceive any of their employees about the use(s) to which personal information held about them will be put.

The second principle: purposes of the data

The duty to obtain data only for one or more specified and lawful purposes, and not process the data for any purpose(s) that is incompatible with those stated purposes

2.3 The second data protection principle requires employers:

- to obtain and use information about individuals only for one or more specified and lawful purposes; and

- not to use the information for any other purposes.

It follows that the employer should firstly be clear as to the (lawful) purpose to be served by the collection of personal information about employees. Then, once an employer has specified the purpose(s) for which they wish to collect information about employees, they must not subsequently use any of the information they hold for any purpose that is incompatible with or vastly different from the purpose for which it was collected.

One example of this principle in practice could be in organisations that use the contact details of their employees (or ex-employees, eg pensioners) for marketing purposes, for example to market the employer's own products or services or advertise any special deals on offer from another organisation. It would not be permissible under the *DPA 1998* to do this without first informing employees that there was an intention to use their personal details for this purpose and giving them a reasonable opportunity to object and decline to have their details used in this way. According to the Employment Practices Code, Part 2 (Employment Records), section 2.6, this can be done in one of two ways:

- by informing new employees if the employer wishes to use their personal details to deliver advertising or marketing information to them and giving them a clear opportunity to 'opt out' by notifying the employer that they do not wish to receive such material; or

- by actively seeking employees' consent to the use of their personal details for this purpose, ie asking them to indicate in writing whether they wish to 'opt in'.

The Code of Practice recommends that employers should:

- ensure that new employees who are to receive marketing information from the organisation have been informed that this will happen;

- give their staff a 'clear opportunity to object (an opt-out) and respect any objections whenever received';

- ensure that the procedure for opting out is clear and made known to all employees.

This matter can sensibly be dealt with during induction by providing each new employee with the information and advising them how to opt out. The employer should, of course, respect any objections and ensure that the details of those persons objecting are not included on any list of names that is to be used for marketing purposes.

Employees should always be given the opportunity to opt out even in circumstances where there is a general expectation that their details will be used for marketing purposes, for example where there is a general, accepted practice in the organisation, or within the particular industry as a whole, of offering staff discounts on the employer's products or services and advertising these to individuals through the use of their personal contact details.

The second method (opting in), according to the Code, should be used in circumstances where the employer wishes to begin marketing or advertising (having not previously carried out any direct marketing to its staff) and employees have not previously been made aware that their personal details might be used in this way. Each employee should be informed of precisely what the employer plans to do and invited to send an email or written note confirming that they wish to opt in. Only those who opt in should have their names put on the marketing list.

A similar approach should be taken in the event that the employer wishes to pass on employees' contact details to another organisation, for example a sister company. The Code of Practice recommends that the employer should put in place a procedure to ensure that no individual's details are passed on until that individual has given a positive indication of their agreement. If this is not done, the disclosure of employees' details to the other organisation would be intrusive and could amount to a breach of the employer's duty of confidence.

The third principle: adequate, relevant and not excessive

The duty to ensure data is adequate, relevant and not excessive in relation to the purpose(s) for which it was obtained

2.4 The third data protection principle states that personal information must be adequate, relevant and not excessive in relation to the purpose or purposes for which it is processed. The employer should therefore regularly carry out reviews of all existing personal data they hold to ensure that the information they keep about their employees in personnel files is not excessive. Essentially, if there is no clear and obvious reason why particular information is being retained in employees' files, the employer should take the appropriate steps to delete or destroy the information.

Another useful action point for employers would be to review carefully all forms and questionnaires they use (for example in recruitment) to check whether the information they request is relevant to the achievement of a legitimate business aim, and is not excessive when viewed in relation to that aim. Any questions that require individuals to provide information that is not strictly relevant and necessary to the employer's needs should be removed or amended. Equally, the wording of the questions should be reviewed to ensure the questions are clear and that they are likely to secure only the information that the employer legitimately requires.

In *Runnymede Borough Council CCRO v The Data Protection Commissioner* (November 1990, unreported), the Data Protection Tribunal, under the 1984 Act (which contained similar provisions), held that where information is required in relation to certain individuals, that does not mean it is reasonable to hold such additional data in relation to *all* individuals.

The fourth principle: accurate and up to date

The duty to ensure personal information is accurate and, where necessary, kept up to date

2.5 The fourth data protection principle obliges employers to ensure personal data is accurate and kept up to date. No employer can ever guarantee that all their staff will automatically cooperate with a request to keep them informed as to any changes to their personal data, for example changes of address, family circumstances or health, but so long as the employer has taken reasonable steps to ensure the accuracy of the information they hold, that should be sufficient to comply with the *DPA 1998*.

One way to increase the chances of personal data being kept up to date is for the employer routinely to issue all the personal data they hold on an annual basis to individuals, and ask for any changes or corrections to be communicated back to the HR department within a given timescale. This approach will have the added advantage that it may reduce the number of subject access requests.

Whether data is inaccurate is a matter of fact in each case. Data is not treated as inaccurate for these purposes where the employee supplied the inaccurate information or a third party did so in circumstances where the employer had taken reasonable steps to ensure the accuracy of the data.

If an employee tells the employer that they believe that the information held about them is inaccurate, then the employer must, at the very least, put a note to that effect in the file.

The fifth principle: how long data should be kept

The duty not to keep personal data for longer than is necessary in relation to the purpose(s) for which it was obtained

2.6 Neither the *DPA 1998* nor the Employment Practices Code prescribes any general time limitation on the retention of personal data. It is therefore up to each employer to decide for themselves what time periods are appropriate in relation to different types of personal information, taking into account the needs of their business. Decisions on this matter should be made objectively, and records should not be maintained 'just in case' they might be needed at some future point in time. Proper policy decisions should be made and adhered to as to the specific retention periods for different types of records, for example the retention of leavers' files (see CHAPTER 6) or recruitment files (see CHAPTER 5).

The length of time over which information should be kept is a difficult and important subject. Some types of records must be held for very long periods. If there is fraud, for example, HM Revenue and Customs can go back to records dating back for longer than the normal six-year period. Where documents are signed as a deed, there is a 12-year limitation period after which legal actions cannot be brought; therefore the documents in this category must be held for at least this period. There are different rules for information such as health and safety records and employee records generally. If the data has only a short-term value to the employer, then it may be appropriate for the information to be deleted after a matter of days or months. The important point is that the employer must analyse the situation and decide what is an appropriate period and what is not in each case.

The Information Commissioner recognises that even where the relationship between the employer and employee has come to an end there may be good reasons for retaining data, for example because a legal action may be mounted against the employer. However only information relevant to the potential claim should be kept and the rest should be destroyed. Once the possibility of a claim has passed then the data should be deleted unless there is another good reason why it needs to be retained.

The sixth principle: processing in accordance with employees' rights

> The duty to process data in accordance with individuals' rights under the DPA 1998

2.7 This is self-explanatory, and would include the duty on the employer to ensure that subject access requests were treated properly and in accordance with the provisions of the *DPA 1998* (see 4.18 below).

The seventh principle: security measures

> The duty to protect personal data by putting in place appropriate technical and organisational measures against unauthorised or unlawful processing, accidental loss or destruction, and damage

2.8 The seventh data protection principle requires employers to put in place proper measures, eg security measures, to protect personal data against unauthorised or unlawful processing, accidental loss or destruction, or damage, taking into account the size and resources of the business and technical and costs factors. This will include adequate protection for computer systems, eg proper use of passwords, and possibly the use of encryption and establishment of firewalls.

One of the simplest and cheapest methods of ensuring the protection of personal data is to formulate and implement a rigorous system of employee passwords. Rules should be devised for employees governing the choosing of a password and for the regular changing of passwords. There should also be a clear written rule forbidding the disclosure of passwords to any unauthorised person, and this rule should be consistently enforced. Disciplinary rules and procedures should make it clear that any unauthorised access to files or misuse of passwords will be regarded as misconduct and render the employee liable to disciplinary action up to and including summary dismissal.

Another simple step that employers can take is to advise all employees that they must not use email, text or fax to communicate personal data. These methods of communication are not secure or confidential. Alternatively, confidential messages that the employer wants to send by email could be encrypted. Encryption simply means the process of translating normal text into a series of letters and/or numbers that can be deciphered only by someone with the correct password or key. It is a useful tool to prevent outsiders from reading confidential, sensitive or personal information.

Employers can further protect employees' personal data by using 'firewalls' and other security technology which can help to keep would-be external hackers at bay to a great extent. The purpose of a firewall is to provide protection against unauthorised access to computer systems and receipt of unwanted correspondence. Technical advice should be sought from computer experts on this subject.

Over and above any breach of the Act, it will be a criminal offence under the *Computer Misuse Act 1990* for an individual to secure unauthorised access to a computer system or to computer material in certain circumstances, or to modify the contents of a computer system without authority. 'Unauthorised modification' of computer material includes deliberate erasure or corruption of programmes or data, modifying or destroying a system file or another user's file or the addition of any programme or data to the computer's contents. It may be advisable for employers to communicate this fact to all staff so that they understand fully the seriousness of any conduct of this nature.

Another point to consider and guard against, in particular in larger organisations, is the possibility of false subject access requests made by an employee in order to gain access to information about another employee for illegitimate or malicious purposes. The employer should put in place the appropriate measures for ensuring that any request for access to an employee's personal file is valid, ie that the identity of the person making the subject access request matches that of the subject of the files requested.

Employers must also take reasonable steps to ensure that staff who have access to personal information during the course of their work are reliable. For example, it would be sensible to take up references before recruiting anyone and check whether they have a police record.

Another advisable security measure is to implement a procedure for cleaning tapes and disks before they are re-used, rather than simply overwriting them. It is safer and better to clean rather than overwrite. If disks are not cleaned, there may be a risk (which should be objectively assessed) that the data may reach someone who is not authorised to have access to it.

Employers also need to assess their waste disposal arrangements. News stories appear on a regular basis about particular banks, building societies or government departments whose waste contractors have for whatever reason dumped confidential papers or disks in a street or at a tip when they should have been disposed of in a more confidential way. The employer should look carefully at the contractual conditions it has with waste disposal companies and ensure that they are strong and well drafted and that they properly address data protection issues.

The following points should be checked:

- Is proper weight given to the assessment of the integrity of staff when they are being considered for employment or promotion, or for a move to an area where they will have access to personal data?

- Are the staff aware of their responsibilities? Have they been given adequate training and is their knowledge kept up to date?

- Do disciplinary rules and procedures take account of the Act's requirements and are they enforced?

- If an employee is found to be unreliable, is their authority to access personal data immediately withdrawn?

- Are passwords known only to authorised persons and are they frequently changed?

- Does a password allow access to all parts of the computer system or just to the personal data with which the employee is concerned? Clearly it is better if there is limited access only, though whether this is possible or practicable will depend on the nature of the employment.

- Will the system keep an audit trail so that all access to personal data can be logged and traced back to an individual?

Where data processing is carried out by another company on behalf of an employer, then the employer must, in order to comply with the seventh data protection principle, choose a company that provides sufficient guarantees in respect of the technical and organisational security measures governing the processing to be carried out and take reasonable steps to ensure compliance with those measures. In other words, the responsibility to comply with the Act remains with the employer even where data processing is contracted out to another organisation. The Act provides that where another company is entrusted with the processing, the employer who owns the data will not be regarded as complying with the seventh principle unless:

- the processing is carried out under a written contract under which the data processor (ie the contractor) is to act only on instructions from the data controller (ie the employer); and

- the contract requires the data processor to comply with obligations equivalent to those imposed on a data controller by the seventh principle.

Paragraph 1.12 above provides further information about the security of personal data.

Should any security breach occur, a full investigation should be carried out.

Employers need to assess the harm which may be caused by particular security breaches. In some cases, very little harm will be caused and in others considerable damage will result: security measures taken should reflect these consequences.

The eighth principle: transfer of data abroad

The duty not to transfer personal data outside the EEA unless the country or territory to which it is transferred has in place an adequate level of protection for individuals' rights and freedoms in relation to the processing of personal data

2.9 The European Economic Area (EEA) consists of all 27 EU countries plus Iceland, Norway and Liechtenstein. The transfer of data to any country or territory outside these countries, for example to the United States, should be subject to the employer satisfying themselves that the data, once transferred, will be properly protected. The *DPA 1998, Schedule 1, para 13* provides that protection must be adequate, having regard in particular to the nature of the personal data; the country of origin of the information; the country of final destination; the purposes for which and period during which the data are intended to be processed; the law in force in the country in question; the international obligations of that country; any relevant codes of conduct or other rules in force in that country; and any security measures taken in respect of the data in that country.

The eighth data protection principle does not apply to data covered by *Schedule 4*. These broad and important exclusions are as follows:

- The data subject (ie the employee) has given consent to the transfer.

- It is necessary in respect of the performance of the employee's contract for the information to be transferred overseas.

- The transfer is necessary to conclude a contract or for the performance of a contract, between the employer and someone other than the employee, which the employee has asked the employer to enter into or which is in the interests of the employee.

- The transfer is necessary for reasons of substantial public interest. The Secretary of State is given powers to formulate orders which set out what may fall within this category.

- The transfer is necessary for the purpose, or in connection with, any legal proceedings including prospective legal proceedings, for the purpose of obtaining legal advice or otherwise necessary for the purposes of establishing, exercising or defending legal rights.

- The transfer is necessary to protect the vital interests of the employee.

- The transfer is of part of the personal data on a public register and any conditions subject to which the register is open to inspection are complied with.

- The transfer is made on terms which are of a kind approved by the Information Commissioner as ensuring adequate safeguards for the rights and freedoms of individuals.

- The transfer has been authorised by the Commissioner as being made in such a manner as to ensure adequate safeguards for the rights and freedoms of individuals.

Chapter 3   Notification

Introduction

3.1   The Information Commissioner maintains a public register of data controllers. Each register entry includes the name and address of the data controller and a general description of the processing of personal data that the data controller undertakes. For an entry to be made, the data controller must notify the Information Commissioner. This is a statutory requirement under the *Data Protection Act 1998*, unless the data controller is exempt. Failure to notify is a criminal offence. According to the Information Commissioner, the principal purpose of the duty of notification and the existence of the public register is transparency and openness. It is a basic principle of data protection that the public should know (or should be able to find out) who is carrying out the processing of personal information as well as other details about the processing (such as for what purpose it is being carried out).

Only one register entry is held for each data controller. It follows that in order that the register entry is complete, the notification must be complete.

Notification lasts for one year and must be renewed each year (unless the data controller no longer has to notify). There is a fee for notification and renewal (see 3.6 below).

As the register is a public document, individuals can consult it to see what processing a data controller does with personal data. It is available online through the Information Commissioner's website at www.ico.gov.uk by following the link to the Information Commissioner's Data Protection Public Register.

A 'Notification Handbook' is provided on the Information Commissioner's website, which is a complete guide to the process of notification (48 pages in length).

Some key points for employers are that:

- Register entries contain a description of the processing of personal data in very general terms.

- Sources of the personal data that the employer processes do not need to be described.

- Transfers of personal data outside the European Economic Area must be described in the notification.

- The notification must contain a statement about the employer's security measures.

- The notification does not need to give an address for the receipt of data subject access requests.

- Some exemptions from notification are provided under the legislation but an employer who is exempt may choose to notify anyway.

What and who needs to be notified?

3.2 The notification must contain details of:

- the data controller (see 3.3 below);

- the purpose or purposes for which data are processed (see 3.4 below);

- to whom the data will be disclosed (see 3.7 below);

- details of transfers outside the European Economic Area (see 3.8 below); and

- a statement about the data controller's security measures (see 3.9 below).

Data controller

3.3 The details required here are the name and address of the employer. The correct legal title of the organisation must be given. In the case of limited companies, including public limited companies and limited liability companies, it must be the full name of the company and not any trading name that may be used. Although these are often the same, trading or business names are governed by the *Business Names Act 1985* and company names by the *Companies Act 1981*. For partnerships, the trading name should be given and it is not necessary to list the names of all the partners.

A group of companies must ensure that each company in the group notifies. There cannot be a single notification for the group as a whole. In practice, it is quite likely that several companies within a group carry out the same or very similar trade and thus will have very similar notifications.

Purposes of processing

3.4 The Information Commissioner provides a list of standard purposes and purpose descriptions for use on the register of data controllers. This list is contained in section 3.1.8 of the 'Notification Handbook' available on the Information Commissioner's website: www.ico.gov.uk. Employers may use their own words to describe a purpose for which they process personal data, but only where none of the descriptions that are provided properly describe the purpose.

Data subjects

3.5 Data subjects are the people about whom the data controller holds information. The Information Commissioner's Notification Handbook (section 3.1.9) provides a set of standard descriptions of data subjects; this is set out in the box below.

By examining this part of the register, a member of the public can establish whether their personal data are likely to be processed by the data controller.

S100	Staff including volunteers, agents, temporary and casual workers
S101	Customers and clients
S102	Suppliers
S103	Members or supporters
S104	Complainants, correspondents and enquirers
S105	Relatives, guardians and associates of the data subject
S106	Advisers, consultants and other professional experts
S107	Patients
S108	Students and pupils
S109	Offenders and suspected offenders

Each description includes past or prospective data subjects as well as current ones. So, for example, S100 will include former employees and job applicants as well as current staff. In the case of deceased employees, the data protection legislation ceases to apply as only living individuals are covered by the Act.

Data classes

3.6 The list of data classes within the register entry specifies the type of personal data that are processed by the data controller. Again, the Information Commissioner's Notification Handbook (section 3.1.10) provides a list of standard descriptions of data classes.

Recipients of data

3.7   Recipients are individuals or organisations to whom the employer intends or may wish to disclose personal data. It does not include any person to whom the employer may be required by law to disclose information, for example if required by the police under a warrant. Again, the Information Commissioner's Notification Handbook (section 3.1.11) provides a standard classification of recipients which include, amongst many others, current, past and prospective employers.

Transfers outside the European Economic Area

3.8   Employers are required to state on their notification whether any transfer of personal data outside the European Economic Area (EEA) takes place.

Merely passing through a country as part of a transfer elsewhere is not deemed to be a transfer. This could occur where a file server is housed in, for example, the Channel Islands and the data are transferred from England to France via that server. However, if the data are stored on the server in the Channel Islands, then the data have been transferred outside the EEA (as the storing of data is processing and the Channel Islands are not part of the EEA).

In the notification, employers must declare the information relating to transfers using one of three options:

● none outside the EEA (if there are none);

● naming up to ten individual countries outside the EEA; or

● worldwide (in all other cases).

If personal data are posted on a website that can be accessed from countries outside the EEA, 'worldwide' should be stated in the notification.

Security measures

3.9   Employers are required as part of the notification to make statements about the security measures that are in place in their organisations. This is done by responding to a number of questions that are asked as part of the notification application. The questions are of a general nature but cover some of the key requirements of effective information security management and can thus be treated as a checklist designed to encourage good information security within the organisation.

This part of the notification is not placed on the public part of the register.

Further information about security measures is contained in 1.12 and 2.8 above.

Exempt processing

3.10 Not all processing of personal data needs to be notified, although register entries must alert anyone examining the register to the fact that processing is taking place that has not been notified. Employers can, if they wish, include in their notification details of all the processing that they do, ie both what has to be notified and that which is exempt from notification. If this is done, then the register entry will be complete and nothing further is required. If, on the other hand, an employer chooses to make use of the exemption and not notify processing where there is no obligation to do so, the notification (and thus the register entry) must contain a statement about exempt processing. The statement is prescribed by the Information Commissioner's Office:

> 'This data controller also processes personal data which are exempt from notification.'

Employers are not required to notify:

- any processing of manual records (although structured manual records are covered by the other provisions of the Act);

- processing for the purpose of staff administration;

- processing for the purpose of advertising, marketing and public relations (in connection with the organisation's own business activity); or

- processing for the purpose of accounts and records.

The expression 'exempt processing' is used in respect of the types of data that are exempt from notification. It is important to remember that an exemption to notify is *not an exemption from the Act*. Paragraph 3.12 below, 'Exemptions from Notification', expands further by discussing the types of organisations that may be exempt altogether from the duty to notify.

Voluntary notification

3.11 All employers are required to notify unless they are exempt from notification. This is discussed at 3.12 below.

An employer who is exempt from notification can nevertheless choose to notify voluntarily. There is a section on the notification form which asks the data controller to indicate whether the notification is voluntary.

Exemptions from notification

3.12 Every data controller who is processing personal information must notify unless there is a relevant exemption from notification. Employers will inevitably be required to notify because they are bound to hold personal information about their workers on file. The Information Commissioner has produced a Notification Handbook containing guidance on the process of notification. The handbook is available on the Information Commissioner's website at: www.ico.gov.uk. Section 6 of the handbook contains a Self-Assessment Guide to Notification Exemptions and provides a list of common purposes that *do* require notification.

Exemptions are possible for:

- some not-for-profit organisations (see 3.13 below for further details);

- those who process personal data for personal, family or household purposes only (including recreational purposes);

- data controllers who process personal data only for the maintenance of a public register;

- data controllers who do not process personal data on a computer (ie only do so manually).

It must be remembered that an exemption to notify is not an exemption from the Act. All data controllers, whether they have to notify or not, must operate within the requirements of the Act.

If any part of an organisation's HR and payroll functions are outsourced to a third party company, that company does not need to notify the processing of its client's personal data. This stems from the concept that the data controller is fully in control of all the processing of the personal data that they choose to gather and process for whatever purpose. If an employer is not processing personal data and not using a computer (or similar equipment capable of automated processing), the employer will be exempt from notification. The very existence of an HR or payroll function in an organisation is, however, a clear indication that personal data are processed. Individuals who process personal data only for their own domestic, family or household purposes are exempt from notifying (and indeed, exempt from the other requirements of the Act). So, a list of friends' and relatives' addresses and dates of birth, even if it was held on a computer, would not create a duty to notify. Similarly, the domestic exemption extends to an individual's recreational activities, such as sports and hobbies.

This provision does not, however, extend to an individual running a business from home as this is beyond the domestic purposes exemption.

Not-for-profit organisations

3.13 Not-for-profit organisations are exempt from the duty to notify provided the processing is limited to the following description.

- The processing is only for the purposes of either establishing or maintaining membership or support for a body or association not established or conducted for profit, or providing or administering activities for individuals who are either members of the body or association or have regular contact with it.

- The data subjects are restricted to any person the processing of whose personal data is necessary for this exempt purpose.

- The data classes are restricted to data that is necessary for this exempt purpose.

- The disclosures other than those made with the consent of the data subjects are restricted to those third parties that are necessary for this exempt purpose.

- The data is retained only until the relationship between the data controller and the data subject ends, unless and for so long as it is necessary to do so for the exempt purpose.

How to notify

3.14   Notification has to be done in writing in the format prescribed by the Information Commissioner. There are three ways of starting the process:

- internet (www.ico.gov.uk: click on 'Notification' in the drop-down box);

- sending (by post or fax) a Notification form (which can be requested online); and

- telephoning the Notification help line at the Information Commissioner's Office on 01625 545 740.

In completing the Request to Notify form, some details of the employer and its business will be given. The same details are requested if the Notification help line is called. The details are used to pre-populate the Notification form that is then sent to the employer. Part 1 of the form needs to be checked and the appropriate sections of Part 2 of the form should then be completed.

Once the details in the notification have been placed on the register, the Information Commissioner's Office will write to the employer enclosing a copy of the register entry. The employer will also be provided with a security number that has to be quoted in all future dealings with the Information Commissioner's Office about the register entry. In effect this is a mechanism to stop people other than the properly authorised person within the employer's organisation from making changes to the register entry.

Fees

3.15 Every notification must be accompanied by a fee of £35.00 (nil VAT).

The period of notification is one year. The Information Commissioner's Office does not send invoices but will acknowledge receipt of payment. A continuation fee of £35.00 must be paid yearly thereafter so long as it is necessary for the employer to remain registered.

It is possible to pay by direct debit, cheque, postal order or BACS.

Amending notification

3.16 Once an entry has been made on the register of data controllers, it may need changing to reflect any changes in the business activities of the organisation. Although notification lasts for only one year and must be renewed annually, there is also an obligation on employers to keep their register entry up to date.

When any part of the register entry becomes inaccurate or the entry is incomplete, the employer must submit the amendment or addition as soon as it is practicable to do so, and in any event within a maximum of 28 days. Failure to do so is a criminal offence.

To amend its register entry, the employer may complete the 'application to alter or remove an entry form' online at the Information Commissioner's website. The security number that was given when the original notification was made will need to be quoted.

No additional fee is payable for amendments. If, however, there is a change in the legal entity of the business, a new entry must be made in the register.

Renewing notification

3.17 Notification lasts for one year only and must be renewed annually, otherwise it will expire. The notification year starts on the day the Information Commissioner's Office receives a complete and correct notification form and the notification fee. The renewal fee is the same as the initial notification fee. A written reminder will be provided by the Information Commissioner's Office before the original notification expires.

Even if there are no changes that have to be made to the register entry, the renewal fee must be received before the old notification expires. For this reason, the Information Commissioner's Office promotes the use of direct debit.

If a notification expires, it cannot be renewed and a new notification must be made.

Once the renewal has been made, the employer will be sent a letter confirming the renewal together with a copy of the renewed entry in the register.

Change of legal entity

3.18 A register entry is not transferable from one employer to another. If there is a change in the legal entity of the employer, a new entry must be made in the register for the new legal entity. The register entry for the old legal entity may then become unnecessary and may need to be removed (see 3.19 below).

If the change is such that a new company number is given to the legal entity by Companies House, a new notification will be needed.

It is recommended that the Notification help line is contacted in the first instance.

Removing the register entry

3.19   If notification ceases to become necessary at any time after an entry has been made on the register of data controllers, the register entry can be removed.

The employer should write to the Information Commissioner's office explaining the change in circumstances and providing its security number. Alternatively, the employer may complete the 'application to alter or remove an entry form' online at the Information Commissioner's website. Any direct debit instruction will also need to be cancelled.

Chapter 4   The Data Protection Act 1998 in practice

Introduction

4.1   The *Data Protection Act 1998* (*DPA 1998*, or 'the Act') was introduced largely to promote openness and transparency of information held about individuals in filing systems, whether manual or computerised, and to protect the privacy of such information. The Act is not an employment law as such, but has considerable impact in every area of the employment relationship.

Personal data

4.2   'Personal data' for the purposes of data protection legislation means simply any personal information held in a filing system that relates to a living individual who can be identified from the data, whether by name or otherwise. This includes information that:

- is held manually (ie on paper) in a 'relevant filing system' (see below);

- is stored in a computer, and information stored in such a way that it can be fed into a computer;

- is contained in the text of an email;

- is stored on microfiche;

- is stored on telephone logging systems, or on audio or video systems; or

- forms part of an 'accessible record'. This would include health records.

In addition, information that is recorded in any format with the intention that it will be put on file or on to computer is regarded as personal data. Where information is stored manually, however, it must be stored in a 'relevant filing system' if it is to fall within the definition of 'personal data'. This means that the file in which the information is stored must be structured in such a way that specific information relating to a particular individual is readily accessible (see also the *Durant* case at 4.3 below).

Information about individuals who are deceased is not covered by the Act.

There is no legal duty on an employer to obtain employees' consent to the collection of personal data, although they must inform employees whenever any record about them is set up or held. There are also further strict rules in place that govern what the employer may, or may not, do with personal data once they have collected it.

In the case of *Pennwell Publishing (UK) Ltd v Isles* [2007] IRLR 700, the High Court had to deal with the question of ownership of a list of contacts that had been maintained on an employer's computer system in circumstances where the list included personal contacts established by the employee prior to his joining the employer. The employee, a journalist, had subsequently left the company, having become involved in a rival business. Before leaving, he copied the entire contacts list for his own future use.

The court ruled that the contact list belonged to the company, but that the employee was entitled when his employment ended to remove the contact details that he had put on to the employer's system to begin with (but not the entire contacts list). This was because, in the absence of an adequately communicated email policy, the employee had not known that these details would, as a result, become part of the employer's property.

The court suggested that it would be 'highly desirable' for employers to devise and publish a clear policy to all employees stating that their email system was to be used only for business purposes and that any information added to the system by an employee would become the employer's property, to be used exclusively for the employer's benefit.

Certain information relating to individuals is regarded as 'sensitive data' under the Act and such data is subject to special provisions and restrictions (see 4.5 below).

The Durant case

4.3   In *Durant v Financial Services Authority* [2003] EWCA Civ 1746, the Court of Appeal held that for a manual record to be part of a 'relevant filing system' for the purposes of the *DPA 1998*, it must be one in which the information is structured by reference to the individual or criteria relating to the individual. The Court pointed out that the purpose of the *DPA 1998* was to protect the privacy of personal data, and not documents. The file must also have a structure or referencing mechanism that allows specific information about the individual to be easily found, eg information about the employee's contract, or on topics such as appraisal, holiday leave or sickness absence. Furthermore, the file must be part of a system in which the files are structured or referenced in a way that specific files about individuals can be readily identified and located within the system without searching through the content of each file.

Following the *Durant* decision, the Information Commissioner subsequently issued guidance and amended the Employment Practices Code. The guidance states that where a filing system contains files about individual employees, or topics about individual employees, and where the files or the information contained within them are structured purely in chronological order, they will not constitute a 'relevant filing system' for the purposes of the Act. This is because the structure or referencing system of the files would not allow the retrieval of personal data without someone having to leaf through the file and search for the data they were looking for. Without some form of indexing or other mechanism to assist with the location of specific data, the file would not be sufficiently structured to fall within the ambit of the Act.

Similarly, where information is filed in a system that uses individuals' names as file names, the system may nevertheless not qualify as a relevant filing system if the indexing, referencing, and/or sub-division is structured otherwise than to allow the retrieval of personal data without leafing through the file.

The Court of Appeal also held in the *Durant* case that in order for information to be 'personal data' for the purposes of the *DPA 1998*, it must not only name or directly refer to an individual, but must also be biographical to a significant extent and have the data subject as its focus (rather than, for example, focusing on some transaction or event in which the individual may have been involved). This would suggest that letters or emails that merely mention an employee's name, for example as one of a list of people who attended a meeting, would not constitute personal data since the individual concerned would not be the focus of the correspondence. In contrast, if the individual's name was mentioned together with other information about them, eg their address, salary details or medical history, it would constitute personal data under the Act. In short, the Court of Appeal took the view that for information to constitute personal data, it must relate in some way to information affecting the individual's privacy, whether in their personal or family life, business or professional capacity.

For example, a filing system in a legal office containing files divided into sections for legal aid, pleadings, orders, correspondence by year, instructions to counsel and counsel's advice, would not be a relevant filing system for the purposes of the DPA because the divisions/referencing would not assist anyone searching through the files to retrieve personal information about an individual without the need to search through the entire file contents.

Data processing

4.4   The *DPA 1998* uses the term 'data processing'. The word 'processing' in this context has a wider meaning than its dictionary definition and covers any and all activities that relate to the collection, holding, use and destruction of information that is about an individual. Thus 'data processing' covers all the routine aspects of handling personal information, including:

- the initial collection of personal information about an individual, howsoever the information is obtained;

- holding the information in a file or on computer;

- organising or reorganising the information;

- making changes to the information, for example as part of an updating exercise, or changing the way in which it is stored;

- retrieving the information, for example as part of a computerised report;

- conveying the information, for example by passing an employee's details to a line manager;

- disclosure of the information by any means or making it publicly available (for example on a company website);

- erasing, deleting or destroying some or all of the information held; and

- using the information in any other way.

Sensitive data

4.5   The *DPA 1998, section 2* sets out a list of personal information which is to be regarded as 'sensitive data'. The list includes the following:

- racial or ethnic origin;

- political opinions;

- religious beliefs or other similar beliefs;

- membership of a trade union;

- physical or mental health or condition;

- sexual life;

- the commission or alleged omission of any offence; and

- anything related to any proceedings for an offence committed or alleged to have been committed.

Information related to a number of the items listed above may in practice be frequently found in an employee's (or job applicant's) file, for example:

- records set up for the purpose of equal opportunities monitoring may contain details of individuals' racial or ethnic origins or religious beliefs;

- a record that an employee of overseas nationality has the right to work in the UK may be held in the individual's file together with copies of documents that prove this right;

- information may be available on file about individuals' trade union membership in order to enable employers to deduct members' subscriptions from their pay at source – it would be reasonable to assume that a written authorisation to deduct subscriptions from pay is also authority to pass the individual's name to the trade union, however it would be against the principles of data protection for a list of union members to be drawn up by the payroll department for distribution to line managers;

- an email from an employee to a trade union representative may reveal that the employee is a member of that trade union;

- sickness records may contain information about an employee's physical or mental health;

- emails sent from an employee to an occupational doctor may contain information about that employee's health or illness;

- personnel files may contain details of an employee's disability and how it affects them so as to enable the employer to meet their duty under the *Disability Discrimination Act 1995* to make reasonable adjustments for that employee;

- an employee's file may contain information about health collected in order to allow the employer to process Statutory Sick Pay – no matter how superficial the data contained in a sick note might be, it is nevertheless data about the physical or mental health of the employee and thus sensitive data;

- information may be contained in an employee's personal file in connection with an allegation of discrimination or harassment, which may reveal that employee's sexual orientation;

- files may contain information about employees' previous criminal convictions where the employee's job involves, for example, security or work of a sensitive nature such as the supervision of children.

Conditions for the processing of sensitive data

4.6   *Schedule 3* of the *DPA 1998* sets out a series of conditions, at least one of which must be met before an employer can process sensitive data about an individual. The conditions that are potentially relevant to data protection in employment are listed below.

- **Where processing is necessary in order for the employer to comply with a legal obligation in connection with employment.**

   Such a legal obligation may arise as a result of statute or common law, ie decisions of courts and tribunals which interpret the law. The scope of this condition is fairly wide and it is the most likely condition to be relevant to the processing of personal data in the context of employment. The condition could apply whether the legal duty in question related to the individual about whom the sensitive data was held, or to another employee. For example, it may be necessary to record details of a particular employee's mental illness in order to be able to ensure the safety of other workers. There are many legal obligations on employers that may require the processing of sensitive data, for example:

   – health and safety legislation;

   – anti-discrimination legislation, including the duty to make reasonable adjustments under the *Disability Discrimination Act 1995*;

   – the duty on public authorities to prohibit sex, race and disability discrimination and promote equality of opportunity in the exercise of their public functions under the *Sex Discrimination Act 1975, section 76A,* the *Race Relations Act 1976, section 71* and the *Disability Discrimination Act 1995, section 49* ;

   – the duty under the *Immigration, Asylum and Nationality Act 2006* to ensure that potential recruits and existing employees have the legal right to work in the UK;

   – the duty under the *Social Security Contributions and Benefits Act 1992* to process Statutory Sick Pay for employees who are absent from work due to sickness;

   – unfair dismissal rights contained in the *Employment Rights Act 1996*;

   – duties and rights under the *Rehabilitation of Offenders Act 1974* which relates to individuals' criminal convictions;

   – the duty to ensure continuity of employment under the *Transfer of Undertakings (Protection of Employment)) Regulations 2006 (SI 2006 No 246)* (the 'TUPE' Regulations) (see 4.12 below).

This list is, of course, not exhaustive.

- **Where processing is necessary to protect the vital interests of the employee or another person in circumstances where the employee cannot give consent.**

    This condition is likely to be satisfied only in cases that represent a matter of life or death.

- **Where the information has been made public as a result of steps taken by the employee.**

    An example of this could be where an employee has taken part in a radio programme in the context of promoting trade union rights, and it is therefore public knowledge that the employee is an active trade union member. In these circumstances, it will not be unlawful for the employer to record the employee's trade union membership and activities on their file.

- **Where processing is necessary in connection with any legal proceedings, including the defence of a legal claim against the employer, or necessary for the purpose of obtaining legal advice.**

    This means that if an employee or job applicant has brought a complaint against their employer to court or tribunal, it would be legitimate for the employer to retain the complainant's personal data (and possibly personal data relating to others) in order to facilitate the employer's defence against the claim. An example could be the retention of a group of job applicants' details, including their respective racial backgrounds, in order to defend a claim of race discrimination brought to tribunal by one of the applicants alleging that their rejection was on racial grounds.

- **Where processing is necessary for the exercise of any functions conferred under an enactment or any functions of the Crown, a Minister of the Crown or a government department.**

    This condition would be relevant mainly to public sector employers who may have special statutory duties conferred on them to ensure the qualifications or probity of employees who fill certain posts. This condition may, for example, justify the processing of information about employees' criminal convictions or any proceedings relating to an offence the employee is alleged to have committed.

- **Where processing is necessary for medical purposes and is undertaken by a health professional or someone with an equivalent duty of confidentiality.**

    This condition would apply where health information about employees was held by a company doctor or similar person (see CHAPTER 7).

- **Where processing of information about individuals' racial or ethnic origin, religious beliefs or physical or mental health is for the purpose of carrying out equal opportunities monitoring.**

If the sole purpose of retaining this type of data is to promote and maintain equality of treatment, and provided the information is necessary in order to achieve this purpose, it will be lawful to retain the data (see CHAPTER 8 for details of equal opportunities monitoring).

One common thread in most of the above conditions is that it must be *necessary* for the employer to hold the sensitive data in order to fulfil the condition. This means that it is not, for example, open to employers to retain sensitive data about individuals in circumstances where the reason for doing so is convenience or 'just in case' a particular situation might arise.

Gaining employees' consent to the processing of sensitive data

4.7   If none of the conditions for processing sensitive data at 4.6 above apply, the only course of action open to an employer who thinks they need to collect and hold sensitive data about an individual is to obtain that individual's consent to the processing of sensitive data. However, under data protection principles, consent to the processing of sensitive data must be 'explicit', and 'freely given'. 'Explicit' in this context means that the employee must have signed a document indicating their agreement, having first been clearly informed how the information will be used. 'Freely given' is defined as giving the employee a genuine choice as to whether or not to consent to the processing, allowing the employee to withdraw consent once given and operating a policy of not subjecting anyone who declines to give their consent to any detriment. Part 4 of the Employment Practices Code (on Health Records) points out that blanket consent obtained at the outset of employment cannot always be relied on.

Despite the fact that it may not always be a sound prospect for an employer to rely on consent as a means of justification for the processing of sensitive data about their employees, it is nevertheless a sensible precaution for an employer as a matter of course to seek employees' (and job applicants') consent to the collection and use of sensitive data about them.

Employers should always consider carefully whether they actually need to collect and hold sensitive data about their employees. If justification exists, they should still aim to keep such data to a minimum. Apart from information gathered for the purpose of equal opportunities monitoring, the only sensitive personal information that the employer is realistically likely to need would be information relating to individuals' trade union membership (for the purpose of deducting subscriptions from wages at source), health, nationality (to comply with the *Immigration, Asylum and Nationality Act 2006*) and (in some, but not all jobs) criminal records.

Individuals' rights under the Data Protection Act

4.8 Employees (and others – see below) have considerable rights under the *DPA 1998*. These can be summarised as follows:

The right to:

- be informed if personal data about them is being processed;
- be given a description of the data;
- be informed of the purpose for which the data is held;
- be told to whom the data may be disclosed and for what purpose (for example disclosure of pay information to the HM Revenue and Customs for taxation purposes);
- have any inaccuracies corrected or removed – if necessary by applying to the courts to obtain an order;
- seek compensation if they have suffered any damage or distress as a result of any breach of the *DPA 1998*;
- prevent processing for the purposes of direct marketing; and
- be given a copy of the information held about them on written request (see 4.18 below).

The rights listed above would be available to:

- employees of the organisation;
- other workers, for example contractors or casual staff where the employer held personal information about them;
- agency staff;
- ex-employees, including pensioners of the company;
- job applicants, whether past or present, successful or unsuccessful;
- volunteer workers;
- apprentices and trainees;
- customers and clients; and
- suppliers.

Individuals' responsibilities under the Data Protection Act

4.9 Data protection issues should not be viewed as the responsibility of only one senior manager within the organisation. Arguably all staff have a duty to comply with the *DPA 1998*, including responsibility for the type of personal data they collect and how they use the information. All workers will have a duty:

- to use personal data to which they have access in the course of their work only for legitimate business purposes;

- to keep personal data about others secure and confidential at all times;

- not to use personal data about others for their own personal purposes; and

- not to disclose personal information about others except when authorised to do so.

It is up to the employer to take the appropriate steps to make sure that all staff, and in particular line managers, understand their responsibilities under the Act and, if necessary, that staff are reminded of these responsibilities from time to time.

In particular, staff should be made aware that they can personally be held liable for a breach of the Act, for example if they knowingly or recklessly disclose personal information outside their employer's organisation without authority to do so. This could be in addition to the employer's liability to pay compensation to any employee who has suffered damage as a result of a breach of the Act (see also CHAPTER 1). Breach of the *DPA 1998* should be quoted as a disciplinary offence in the employer's disciplinary procedure in order to draw to the attention of all staff to the fact that the employer views such breaches seriously.

A useful way of achieving these objectives would be for the employer to prepare written rules and guidelines to be distributed to line managers and others whose jobs take them into contact with personal data, explaining the key duties and responsibilities under the Act and the consequences of individuals' actions.

Technology

4.10   With the advent of advances in technology, the risk of personal information about individuals being inadvertently recorded, used and/or disclosed has risen considerably. Many employees nowadays use laptops, palmtops and blackberries in the course of their work and these devices may contain personal data, including sensitive data, about individuals. It is therefore extremely important that employers' policies address the use of these devices and state clearly what uses are, and are not, permitted. Measures should also be in place to ensure the prompt return of all electronic equipment belonging to the employer when an employee leaves and to have it checked over by a responsible person before being reallocated to another employee.

Mobile phones represent a particular risk for employers. Many employees bring their personal mobile phones into the workplace and employers may need to exercise a reasonable degree of control over how, when and where they are used. Most mobile phones can, for example, take photographs. A photograph of an employee at work will constitute personal data about that person and it is unlikely where such a photograph is taken casually that the principles of the DPA will have been adhered to. A simple solution to this risk is for employers to apply some basic rules on the use of personal mobile phones in the workplace, including a prohibition on the taking of any photographs at work unless express permission to do so had been given by management.

Legal requirement to disclose personal data about employees

4.11   As a general principle, employers are obliged to keep employees' personal data secure and confidential and not disclose it other than to authorised persons. There are, however, a number of exceptions to this general principle where the employer may be required by law to disclose personal data relating to their employees to outside bodies or agencies. The organisations to whom such disclosures must be made on demand would include the:

* HM Revenue and Customs;

* Child Support Agency;

* Benefits Agency;

* Department of Work and Pensions; and

* Financial Services Authority.

There are a number of legal duties on employers to disclose information about their workers to outside bodies and agencies. Prior to doing so, however, the employer should check that there really is a legal duty to do so. Assuming that this has been established, the employer should still only provide the information that they are legally obliged to disclose and no more. Furthermore, in normal circumstances the employee concerned should be immediately informed that a disclosure has been made, to whom it has been made, why it has been made and what information about him or her has been disclosed.

An employer may be approached by the police asking to be given data about an employee. The natural inclination of most HR managers would be to cooperate with the police. It may, however be better to take advice on the appropriateness of the approach in case the employee's rights under the *DPA 1998* are breached as a result of a disclosure and the employer is held liable.

Having said that, the employer should take into account that the objective of preventing or detecting crime would override the employee's rights not to have information about him/her disclosed to the police. Personal data that is processed for the purpose of preventing or detecting crime is exempt from the non-disclosure provisions of the Act in circumstances where a decision not to disclose would be likely to prejudice that purpose. This exemption does not, however, mean that there is an obligation on the employer to disclose, but rather that a disclosure may be made without the employer being in breach of the Act. The Employment Practices Code points out that there must be a 'substantial chance, rather than a mere risk' that the police enquiry would be prejudiced by a failure to disclose.

It would be advisable for the employer in these circumstances to ensure that any decision is taken at an appropriately senior level within the organisation and for the reasons for it to be clearly documented.

Payroll departments frequently receive requests from third parties to provide information about an employee's earnings, for example a request from a mortgage lender to confirm an individual's level of pay. There is no legal obligation upon the employer to provide the requested information in such cases, and any disclosure of information about an employee's level of earnings would contravene the data protection legislation unless the employee had asked for, or expressly consented to, the data being disclosed.

There is also a legal duty under the *Transfer of Undertakings* (*Protection of Employment*) *Regulations 2006* for employers to disclose certain defined information about employees in the event that their employment is to be transferred to a new employer (see 4.12–4.16 below).

Data protection and transfers of undertakings

4.12 The *Transfer of Undertakings* (*Protection of Employment*) *Regulations 2006* (*SI 2006 No 246*), known as TUPE, were introduced to protect employees in the event that the organisation for which they work changes hands.

What is a transfer of an undertaking?

4.13 The question of whether a transfer of an undertaking has occurred is a complex one and is outside the scope of this book. Broadly, TUPE will be activated when:

- a business is sold and the new owners continue the same or a similar type of business as before;

- two or more businesses are merged;

- there is a management buy-out;

- a lease or franchise is granted or transferred;

- a defined activity, eg payroll, cleaning, etc is contracted out or outsourced;

- a contract is discontinued and the relevant activities taken back in-house;

- a service contract changes hands, ie the employer decides (usually following a tendering exercise) not to renew a contract with the existing contractor but to award it to a different contractor instead.

The key feature of TUPE is that in any of the above situations, the employees engaged in the undertaking (or the part of the undertaking) that is transferred will automatically become employees of the new employer on the date the transfer takes place. The new employer is thus obliged in law to employ all the employees who were employed in the business (or part of the business) that is being transferred.

TUPE provides for employees' contracts of employment to transfer auto-matically from the original employer (the transferor) to the new employer (the transferee) and to continue as if they had originally been made with the new employer. This has the effect that employees' statutory and contractual rights automatically become enforceable against the new employer. All the rights, duties and liabilities connected with the relevant employees' contracts transfer across to the new employer by operation of law, with the exception of some benefits under occupational pension schemes and any outstanding criminal liabilities.

TUPE creates a number of rights for employees affected by a transfer, which can be summarised as follows:

- the right to have their service with the new employer treated as having begun on the date they commenced employment with the original employer;

- the right to continue in employment with the new employer on the same contractual terms and conditions of employment as applied under the original employer;

- the right not to be dismissed because of the transfer or for a reason related to the transfer, unless (in the latter situation only) there is an 'ETO reason' for the dismissal (which means an 'economic, technical or organisational reason entailing changes in the workforce');

- the right to be informed and consulted about the transfer.

The duty to notify employee liabilities

4.14 One of the key duties under TUPE (and the area that is affected by the *DPA 1998*) is for the original employer to give the new employer written notice of all transferring rights and obligations in relation to the employees who are going to transfer. This information is known as 'employee liability information' (see 4.15 below). Because the law requires certain information to be supplied by the original employer to the new employer, it is not necessary for the original employer to seek the employees' consent.

What information must be provided?

4.15 Because employee liability information must be provided to the new employer in writing, it falls within the scope of the *DPA 1998*. The information that must be provided is as follows:

- the identity (ie the names) of the transferring employees, and their ages;
- information contained in the transferring employees' written statements of particulars of employment;
- information about any collective agreements that apply to the transferring employees;
- details of any disciplinary action taken against any of the transferring employees during the previous two years;
- any formal grievances raised by any of the transferring employees during the previous two years;
- details of any legal action brought against the original employer in any court or employment tribunal by any of the transferring employees during the last two years, and of any potential legal action that the employer reasonably believes might be brought.

Additionally, if there are changes to the information between the date it was provided and the date of the transfer, the original employer must provide the new employer with the necessary updates.

TUPE requires the necessary information to be supplied at least two weeks before the completion of the transfer unless special circumstances make this not reasonably practicable (in which case the information must be provided as soon as possible).

Where the original employer has failed to provide the requisite information to the new employer, the new employer may complain to an employment tribunal. If the complaint is successful, the tribunal can order the original employer to award compensation to the new employer for any loss suffered, subject to a standard *minimum* amount of £500 per employee.

It is not permitted for the two employers involved in a TUPE transfer to agree to contract out of the duty to provide employee liability information.

Good practice guidelines

4.16 Employers involved in a TUPE transfer should take care to comply with the data protection principles when handling the relevant personal information. Further advice on the disclosure of employee liability information under TUPE is available on the Information Commissioner's website: www.ico.gov.uk.

The original employer should:

- consult the new employer on the method to be used to provide the required information;

- inform the employees who are to transfer that their information will be passed to the new employer;

- ensure the information provided to the new employer about the transferring employees is accurate and up to date;

- ensure the transfer of the information to the new employer is subject to appropriate security measures;

- if information about employees is requested that does not fall within the scope of TUPE, supply such information in an anonymised form if possible, or alternatively obtain the relevant employees' consent to its disclosure;

- retain personal information about the employees transferred (after the transfer) only for as long as this is necessary to fulfil a legitimate business purpose, for example to deal with any outstanding liabilities.

The new employer should:

- consult the original employer on the method to be used to provide the required information;

- use the information supplied by the original employer only for the purposes of TUPE, for example to assess possible liabilities or make plans as to how the new employees will be integrated into their business;

- ensure the information supplied by the original employer is treated as confidential and is subject to appropriate security measures;

- review the information supplied, consider whether it is all needed and delete or destroy any information that is not needed for the purpose of the individuals' ongoing employment.

Key features of the Employment Practices Code

4.17   The Employment Practices Code was originally published in four separate parts by the Information Commissioner. The Code was subsequently consolidated and re-published as a single document, available on www.ico.gov.uk. There is also Supplementary Guidance providing further details on the Code's recommendations. The Code represents the Information Commissioner's interpretation of the steps employers should take to ensure compliance with the *DPA 1998*. In addition to sections about the Code and how to manage data protection generally, it consists of four parts which are:

- Part 1: Recruitment and selection – This covers personal data held in the context of recruitment, including carrying out checks on job applicants (see CHAPTER 5);

- Part 2: Employment records – This covers a range of information about staff likely to be held on file by employers (see CHAPTER 6);

- Part 3: Monitoring at work – This covers mainly monitoring of employees' communications but also some other forms of monitoring (see CHAPTER 9);

- Part 4: Information about workers' health– This covers occupational health data, medical testing, drugs screening and genetic testing (see CHAPTER 7).

Neither the *DPA 1998* nor the Code of Practice prevents employers from processing data about employees. Instead they set out to ensure that employers process personal data in a fair and proper way and regulate when and how processing is carried out. The key stated aims of the Code of Practice are to:

- help employers to comply with the *DPA 1998* and encourage them to adopt good practice in the handling of personal data; and

- strike a balance between an employer's legitimate interests in deciding how best to run its business and the legitimate expectations of workers that personal information about them will be handled properly.

The Code, like other Codes of Practice, is not legally binding on employers, but a failure to follow its recommendations can be used in evidence against an employer in the event of a court or tribunal claim. It is therefore in every employer's interests to adhere to the recommendations given in the Code, which in any event is a useful source of information and practical guidance in an area that can sometimes be quite complex.

The Code of Practice identifies a range of examples of the types of personal information that would be likely to be covered by the provisions of the *DPA 1998*, including:

- details of a named employee's pay and bank account details, whether held manually or on computer;

- an email about an incident involving a named member of staff;

- information written in a supervisor's notebook about an employee where the supervisor planned to put that information into the employee's personnel file;

- an individual's personnel file provided it is structured in such a way that specific information can be readily accessed;

- a set of cards where each employee has an individual card and the cards are kept in alphabetical order; and

- a set of completed job application forms filed in alphabetical order within a file of application forms for a particular job vacancy.

Examples of information that would be unlikely to be covered by the Act are also given in the Code of Practice:

- information about the employer's salary structure and grading system where no individuals were named;

- a report on the comparative success of different recruitment campaigns where no details of any individual job applicants were included;

- a report on the results of 'exit interviews' where the individual responses were anonymised and impossible to trace back to individuals; and

- a personnel file containing information about a named employee in which the various pieces of information were filed in date order with nothing in the file to indicate where specific information could be found (ie with no indexing or other similar structure).

These lists are of course intended to be illustrative and not exhaustive. Essentially, whenever a record is created about an individual (or the individual's activities), it is liable to fall within the scope of the *DPA 1998* and the Code of Practice.

The Code points out that in general, information will be covered by the Act and the Code of Practice if an individual can be identified (whether by name or by other means, for example a reference number). Where, however, information is held about a group of people in such a way that individuals are not named or otherwise identifiable, the information will not constitute personal data, and hence will not be covered by either the Act or the Code of Practice.

Requests for access to employees' personal files

4.18   One of the cornerstones of the Act is that it gives individuals the right to contact any organisation that they believe holds information about them personally and request access to that information. Such a request is known as a 'subject access request'. Requests for access may be made in respect of manual files, microfiche records, audio or video tapes, computer files and email correspondence that contains information about the individual. The individual making the subject access request is not obliged under the Act to give any reason for seeking the information.

The right of access relates strictly only to data held about the employee making the subject access request. Employers should not under any circumstances disclose third party data to an individual. Even if, for example, a parent makes a request for information about an employee who is their son or daughter, they must not be given any personal information about the employee.

A fee of up to £10 per access request may be charged if the employer so chooses. Many employers will, in practice, grant their employees one free subject access request per year, but then charge £10 for any or all further requests within the same year. This approach strikes a reasonable balance, ie it allows employees to see, at regular intervals, what information the employer holds about them on file, without creating a situation where the employer might otherwise be inundated with frequent requests for access to data, compliance with which could be time-consuming and disruptive.

The Act lays down strict rules as to how subject access requests should be made and dealt with. For a subject access request to be valid, it must be in writing (email is acceptable) and must identify the data to which the person seeks access.

When an employer receives a subject access request, they should:

- verify the identity of the person requesting access to the data, if necessary (ie to ensure that personal information is disclosed only to the person who is its subject);

- inform the person making the application if the employer does in fact keep any personal information about them, and if so provide a description of the type of information held, the purposes for which the information is used and to whom it may be disclosed;

- inform the person making the application whether a fee is to be charged for the provision of a copy of the information;

- (once any fee has been paid and identity verified) produce copies of the relevant information in an intelligible permanent form promptly and at least within 40 calendar days and provide these to the individual. If any codes or reference numbers are used, an explanation of these should be provided; and

- give the employee any additional information that the employer has about the sources of the information provided (unless this would involve the unauthorised disclosure of confidential information relating to another individual).

The employer is not obliged to comply with an employee's request for access unless the employee has supplied such information as the employer may reasonably require in order to locate the information requested. In the event of an unspecific request, the employer would be advised to ask the employee to limit their request by defining it in some way, for example by date range, or by specifying authors, recipients or subject matter.

The employer may refuse to comply with a subject access request if the same employee has previously made a similar or identical request and a 'reasonable time interval' has not yet elapsed between compliance with the previous request and the making of the current request. 'Reasonable time interval' is, however, not defined in the Act and so a common sense approach should be taken.

As a result of these provisions, employees have the right to see documents such as:

- performance reviews or appraisals;

- sickness records;

- warnings or minutes of disciplinary interviews;

- training records;

- statements about pay;

- emails or word-processed documents of which they are the subject; and

- expressions of opinion about (for example) promotion prospects.

Employees may also request access to information generated by computer systems involved in automated decision making on matters such as performance and conduct.

In requesting access to personal data held about themselves, employees may seek access to copies of any emails in which their name appears.

Employees will not, however, usually be entitled to be granted access to all emails just because they were the sender or recipient, although access would normally have to be granted to emails in which the employee was the subject of the email. If the employee's name was merely mentioned in the email, for example as one of a list of people who attended a meeting, it is unlikely that disclosure would be required under the Act.

It would be advantageous for employers to:

- nominate a senior person in the organisation who is to be responsible for ensuring that subject access requests are properly dealt with;

- establish a system and procedure for responding to subject access requests, including how any requirement for employees to pay a fee for subject access will be administered;

- ensure that all information is readily accessible; and

- create a checklist that lists the locations where personal data is held.

Exceptions to an employee's right of access to personal data

4.19   There are some limited exemptions to the general duty to comply with a subject access request. These include circumstances where the information held relates to:

- management planning or forecasting;

- negotiations with employees;

- the price of a company's shares;

- the prevention or detection of crime or the apprehension or prosecution of offenders;

- the assessment or collection of any tax or duty;

- references; and

- data about another person.

A partial exemption also exists where the provision of a permanent copy of the information requested would require disproportionate effort.

These exemptions are discussed further at 4.20–4.27 below.

Information relating to management planning

4.20   Information relating to management planning or forecasting may be withheld if its disclosure would be likely to prejudice the employer's business. Examples of the type of information that could potentially be withheld under this heading would be plans to promote or transfer an employee, or a proposal to make a group of staff redundant. Employers should note, however, that employers may be under a statutory duty to consult employees over proposed redundancies, depending on the numbers of staff involved.

Negotiations with employees

4.21 If the employer has information on file that, if disclosed, would reveal its intentions in relation to negotiations with an employee, a group of employees, workers' representatives or a trade union, and if such a disclosure would be likely to prejudice the negotiations, the information may be withheld. An example could be information that stated how far the employer was prepared to go in forthcoming or current pay negotiations.

Information on the price of a company's shares

4.22 This limited exemption (known as the 'corporate finance exemption') could apply where disclosure of information might affect the price of a company's shares or other financial instrument.

Information held for the prevention or detection of crime

4.23 Employers would be entitled to refuse to disclose personal information about an employee to that employee if the disclosure would be likely to prejudice the prevention or detection of crime or the apprehension or prosecution of an offender.

Information held for the assessment or collection of any tax or duty

4.24 Refusal to disclose personal data under this heading would be legitimate if the grounds for the refusal were similar in principle to those given at 4.23 above, ie if disclosure would be likely to prejudice the legitimate collection of income tax or other tax or duty.

References

4.25 There is an exemption in respect of references given in confidence in relation to the organisation that gave the reference. Such references may be for the purpose of the person's employment (a job reference), appointment to any office, their education or training, or for the purpose of any service to be provided to the person.

The exemption for references no longer applies, however, once the reference is in the hands of the recipient employer. Thus references contained in employees' or job applicants' files are subject to disclosure, but may nevertheless be withheld on the grounds that the reference would reveal information about a third party (see 4.26 below).

Data that would reveal information about a third party

4.26 A general exemption applies to any information the disclosure of which would reveal information about another person (a third party), such that the third party could be identified from it. Disclosing the document could in some cases lead to a breach of confidence and a violation of the third party's rights under the *DPA 1998*. Examples of such information could include a written statement of complaint about an employee, signed by a colleague, or a confidential job reference received from another employer and signed by an individual manager. In this case, the employer should first of all consider whether either of the following options would be a reasonable course of action:

- to request permission from the third party to release the document to the employee who has requested it; or

- to blank out the details of the third party before making the document available to the employee who has requested it (if doing so would be sufficient to conceal their identity).

The case of *Asda Stores Ltd v Thompson* [2004] IRLR 598 endorses the approach suggested above of blanking out the third party's identity from a document. In this case, the Employment Appeal Tribunal ruled that, for the purpose of disposing of the employee's complaint of unfair dismissal, the employer had to disclose confidential witness statements involving allegations of drugs dealing, but that they could conceal the identity of the witnesses, or if necessary edit parts of the statements, in order to prevent the witnesses from being identified.

Before refusing to release a document that would disclose details of a third party, the employer should take a reasoned decision on whether it is reasonable to disclose it, by balancing the third party's right to privacy against the employee's right to know what information is held about them and its source.

Employers should bear in mind, however, that even though a third party may be identified in a document to which an employee has requested access, the information may not be confidential. If, for example, the document states facts of which the employee is already aware, then there would be no valid reason to refuse disclosure of the document to the employee notwithstanding that it contained the names of one or more third parties.

The Supplementary Guidance to Part 2 of the Employment Practices Code (Employment Records) endorses this point by suggesting that the release of references that contain only factual information about the individual, such as their sickness record, would be unlikely to be in breach of the Act and that employers should normally be prepared to disclose information that identifies work colleagues, provided the colleagues provided the information in a business capacity and so long as the information is not of a particularly private or sensitive nature.

Factors that employers should consider when conducting the balancing exercise in order to decide whether to permit access are:

- whether the disclosure of the document as it stands would actually be in breach of the duty of confidence owed to the third party – automatic assumptions about this should be avoided;

- whether the information identifies the third party in a business or personal capacity – the right to privacy will be greater if the third party is identifiable in a personal capacity, for example where a personal, rather than a corporate, reference has been provided;

- the nature of the information and whether its disclosure could potentially be damaging to the third party, for example if the document contained a complaint about the employee made by a colleague, the colleague may fear (reasonably or unreasonably) that the employee might seek revenge on them if their identity as the author of the complaint was disclosed;

- whether the information is already known to the employee either in total or in part, in which case the release of the document should not risk being in breach of the duty of confidence owed to the third party;

- whether the documents contain information that the employee would have a right to know or would have a right to dispute, for example allegations about poor job performance or misconduct;

- whether it is feasible to edit the document in such a way as to remove the identity of the third party without significantly changing its content or relevance to the employee who requested access to it (for example the employer should consider whether it is possible to photocopy the document in such a way that the third party's name does not appear on the copy);

- whether the third party has expressly refused consent to the disclosure of the document, and if so the reasons given and whether they are considered reasonable;

- what information the third party was given when consent was requested, and what their reasonable expectations would be, for example it would not be appropriate to take the view that references can be kept confidential in all circumstances since a court or tribunal can order their disclosure where they consider that it is in the interests of justice to do so;

- the impact the disclosure of the information might have on the employee, for example whether disclosure would be likely to have a negative or damaging effect on them.

Disproportionate effort

4.27 A partial exemption to the duty to respond to a subject access request exists in circumstances where the provision of a permanent copy of the information requested would require disproportionate effort. Even if this is the case, however, the employer must do all they reasonably can to provide the employee with access to the information they have requested, for example by allowing them to inspect a file rather than providing a copy of everything in the file. Alternatively, the employer may be able to deal with the problem effectively by asking the employee to redefine their request, for example to specify a date range for a set of documents, specify authors or recipients of information, or provide more detail of the subject matter of the data that they wish to access.

The *DPA 1998* does not define 'disproportionate effort' but it is likely that matters affecting what would or would not be disproportionate could include:

- the time needed to locate all the information requested by the individual;

- the cost of providing the information in permanent form; and

- any particular difficulty involved in locating or providing the information.

Employers should only decline to provide an employee with a permanent copy of the files requested on the basis of the disproportionate effort exemption in exceptional circumstances. A better course of action would be to provide as much information as the employer reasonably can and explain why the remainder of the information requested is delayed, or cannot be provided.

An example of this provision coming into play could be if an employee requested access to all the emails on the employer's computer system that contained information about him or her. It would in all likelihood be an unwieldy task to search through all the company's email records just in case there might be a message that contained information about the employee in question. This would involve disproportionate effort. The employer should, however, check locations that are reasonably likely to contain emails about the employee, the most obvious example being the employee's line manager's inbox and outbox. Alternatively, the employee could be asked to provide more information as to the likely location of any email messages, so that the search could be narrowed down.

Chapter 5   Data protection in recruitment and selection

Introduction

5.1 The recruitment and selection of new staff represents one of the most important activities of any organisation. An organisation that attracts and retains talented people will in all likelihood perform well. In contrast, if recruitment is not carried out effectively and within the law, the results can be poor performance, the need for increased supervision, excessive training, frustration for the colleagues of the new recruit, and ultimately the possibility that the employer will have to dismiss the new employee and begin the recruitment process all over again.

The key aim of this chapter is to explore the subject of recruitment in light of the data protection provisions contained in the *Data Protection Act 1998* (*DPA 1998* or 'the Act') and the Employment Practices Code, Part 1: Recruitment and Selection (the Code of Practice).

Creating and maintaining records of job applicants

5.2 The recruitment process will inevitably lead to the need to create a set of records for each job applicant and to maintain these records throughout the process of recruitment and for at least a short period of time after the recruitment exercise has been concluded. Some of the data held on file will be information provided by the job applicant, whilst other papers will be those created by the employer. Relevant documents may include:

- the applicant's CV and/or application form;
- letters from the employer to the job applicant acknowledging the person's application, inviting them to interview and providing a response post-interview;
- letters from the applicant to the employer relating to interview arrangements;
- a copy of the job description and employee specification;
- interview notes made at or after the interview (see 5.19 below);
- copies of any psychometric or other tests completed by the applicant and their results/interpretation;

- personal information about the applicant's racial or ethnic background, obtained for monitoring purposes (see 5.17 below);

- interview expense claim forms;

- references obtained about the applicant from third parties (see 5.25 below);

- medical information about the applicant, for example a medical questionnaire completed by the applicant or a report from an occupational doctor (see 5.18 below);

- copies of certificates or proof of qualifications supplied by the job applicant (see 5.28 below);

- copies of documents that prove the individual has the right to work in the UK (required under the *Immigration, Asylum and Nationality Act 2006*) (see 5.29 below);

- statements from the Criminal Records Bureau or Disclosure Scotland concerning any criminal records appertaining to the applicant (see 5.30 below);

- a copy of a letter from the employer offering the individual employment, and a copy of the applicant's acceptance or rejection;

- a written statement of the individual's key terms and conditions of employment.

Not of all of the above documents will constitute 'personal data' under the Act; for example the job description and employee specification will not be specific to any one job applicant.

The extent to which information held about job applicants constitutes 'personal data'

5.3 If some or all of the information created about a job applicant is input to a computer, it will automatically constitute personal data, defined in the *DPA 1998* as 'data which relate to a living individual who can be identified either from the data, or from the data together with other information which is in the possession of the data controller.'

If, as is more likely, the information is held manually, it will fall under the Act if it is contained in a 'relevant filing system'. A relevant filing system is a set of information that is 'structured, either by reference to individuals or by reference to criteria relating to individuals, in such a way that specific information relating to a particular individual is readily accessible'.

In *Durant v Financial Services Authority* [2003] EWCA Civ 1746, (see also 4.3) the Court of Appeal interpreted the scope of this provision quite narrowly. The Court stated that, in order for information held manually to be 'personal data' for the purposes of the Act, it must not only name or directly refer to an individual, but must also be biographical to a significant extent and have the data subject as its focus. The Court of Appeal took the view that for information to constitute personal data, it must relate in some way to information affecting the individual's privacy, whether in their personal or family life, business or professional capacity. This would suggest, for example, that letters sent between the employer and the applicant concerning interview arrangements would not necessarily constitute personal data since the focus of the letters would be the interview arrangements and not the applicant.

Despite the *Durant* decision, it is advisable for employers to assume in the first instance that much of the information held on file about a job applicant will fall within the scope of the Act and thus be subject to the subject access provisions (see 5.5 below).

Information about a job applicant that constitutes 'sensitive data'

5.4   Clearly records appertaining to job applicants should be treated as strictly confidential. Some of the data in the applicant's file may constitute 'sensitive data' under the *DPA 1998*, defined as:

'personal data consisting of information as to:

(a)   racial or ethic origin;

(b)   political opinions;

(c)   religious beliefs or other beliefs of a similar nature;

(d)   whether the person is a member of a trade union;

(e)   physical or mental health or condition;

(f)   sexual life;

(g)   the commission or alleged commission of any offence;

(h)   any proceedings for any offence committed or alleged to have been committed, the disposal of such proceedings or the sentence of any court in such proceedings.'

Some of the information gathered during the recruitment process may qualify as sensitive data such as:

•   information about the applicant's health, or disability, obtained as a result of a pre-employment medical examination or following the completion by the applicant of a medical questionnaire;

- information about criminal convictions or other information obtained from the Criminal Records Bureau or Disclosure Scotland in respect of the applicant;

- information that reveals the applicant's nationality (and hence racial origins) obtained for the purpose of proving their right to work in the UK;

- information provided for monitoring purposes on the applicant's racial or ethic origin.

The issue of sensitive data in relation to job applications is explored further at 5.13 below.

Job applicants' right of access to records

5.5 Job applicants about whom information is held on a file by a prospective employer will have the right to request access to the information held about them, subject to the request for access being in writing (email is acceptable) and to the payment of any fee prescribed by the employer (up to a maximum of £10). This is known as a subject access request. A job applicant will have the right to submit a subject access request irrespective of whether their application was in response to a job advertisement or unsolicited, and irrespective of whether the application has been successful or unsuccessful. So long as a record about the job applicant still exists, the person will have the right of access to it. In the event of a valid request, the employer must comply by providing the job applicant with:

- a description of the type of information held about the applicant, the purpose(s) for which it is held and any types of organisation that the information may be passed on to;

- a copy of the data itself in permanent and intelligible form.

This information must be provided promptly and within a timescale of no more than 40 calendar days.

The right of access may include access to information about the applicant contained in the text of emails, for example internal emails from an HR officer to the line manager of the department in which the vacancy exists providing information about the applicant. By contrast, an email that simply listed the names of a group of job applicants would not constitute personal data.

Requests for access to data must be sufficiently precise to enable the employer to locate the right information, otherwise, under the principle of proportionality, the employer will not be obliged to comply (see 4.27

above). In the case of requests for access from job applicants, it would not be difficult for the applicant to make their subject access request precise. It is likely that it would be sufficiently precise for the applicant to identify the job vacancy (for example by referring to the job title or any reference number provided by the employer) and the date their application was submitted and state that they were seeking access to any file containing personal information about them in relation to recruitment into that job.

If any of the information held in the recruitment file identifies a third party, the employer must take care not to breach that third party's rights under the Act. The most obvious example of this would be in relation to any references held on the applicant's file provided in confidence by a previous employer or other contact which would, if disclosed, reveal the identity of the author of the reference. Paragraph 5.26 below deals fully with this issue.

The Code of Practice on Recruitment

5.6 The Information Commissioner has published an Employment Practices Code, part 1 of which deals specifically with recruitment and selection. There is also a detailed Supplementary Guidance to the Code (the Guidance).

The Code of Practice is not legally binding, but represents the Information Commissioner's recommendations as to how employers should fulfil their legal requirements under the Act in relation to data protection. In the event of a legal challenge, however, a court or tribunal can take the Code of Practice into account, and evidence of non-compliance can operate to the employer's detriment. One key stated aim of the Code of Practice is to: 'strike balance between the legitimate expectations of workers that personal information about them will be handled properly and the legitimate interests of employers in deciding how best, within the law, to run their own businesses'. Much of the Code is concerned with proportionality, ie whether a particular course of action carried out by the employer is appropriate and necessary for the achievement of a legitimate aim when balanced against the needs of the individual, including the right to privacy.

The Code of Practice provides guidance on every stage of the recruitment process from advertising the job through to the retention of recruitment records. Some of the general principles advocated by the Code of Practice are that employers should:

- disclose the organisation's identity to all job applicants as soon as possible (for example if the post is advertised via an employment agency);

- restrict the information they collect about job applicants to that which is relevant to the job in question;

- refrain from collecting information about job applicants' personal lives unless it is necessary for the purpose of the specific recruitment exercise;

- collect sensitive data only where the job applicant's explicit consent has been obtained or in circumstances where the collection of such data is in order to fulfil a legal obligation (for example a check carried out via the Criminal Records Bureau in relation to a post involving the supervision of children or vulnerable adults);

- inform job applicants as to how the information held about them is to be used unless this is self-evident;

- ensure any tests used as part of the assessment process are carried out by properly trained and qualified personnel;

- retain recruitment records for as short a period of time as necessary, based on business needs;

- notify the applicant if the employer wishes to retain their details on file after the conclusion of the recruitment exercise, explaining how the information will be used and how long it will be kept, and giving the applicant the option to ask the employer not to retain it;

- ensure the security of all job applications, including devising a secure method for individuals to send in their applications online;

- not automatically transfer all the data relating to the recruitment of the successful job applicant to a permanent employee file, but instead transfer only the data that is relevant and necessary for the ongoing employment relationship.

Part 1 of the Code does not deal in detail with health information on job applicants, as this is covered by Part 4 of the Code (see CHAPTER 7).

The points listed above are explored further in the following sections.

Ensuring advertising complies with data protection provisions

5.7   The Code of Practice identifies a number of key actions required of employers in relation to job advertising. The underlying principle is that the advertising process should be open and transparent, making it clear to anyone who may wish to respond to the employer's advertisement how the information they supply will be used and to whom it may be disclosed.

The key principles contained in the Code of Practice relating to job advertising are that employers should:

- identify themselves in the advertisement rather than (for example) providing only a PO box number for replies or a website address that does not make it clear who the employer is;

- inform job applicants as soon as possible of how the information supplied by them will be used in circumstances where the employer intends to use such information for any purpose other than recruitment into the post in question, for example if the employer intends to pass on applicants' details to another organisation or use it for marketing purposes. This is in line with the second data protection principle which requires employers to obtain personal data only for one or more specified and lawful purposes and not to process personal data in any manner incompatible with those purposes.

The Guidance suggests that an advertisement placed by a recruitment agency need not show the identity of the employer on whose behalf it is recruiting, but that the employer should, as soon as possible, take steps to inform each applicant of their identity and how they intend to use the applicant's details (unless this is self-evident). This information can be supplied directly to applicants or the task delegated to the recruitment agency to pass the information on to the applicants.

Where an employer wishes to remain anonymous to job applicants until a later stage in the recruitment process, they may do so only if they arrange to receive candidates' applications from the recruitment agency in an anonymous form. In this way, fairness is maintained because neither party will know the identity of the other unless and until the employer decides to take forward an individual's application to the next stage of the recruitment process, at which time they should disclose their identity to the applicant.

Advertising by recruitment agencies

5.8 Where the organisation placing the job advertisement is a recruitment agency, the Guidance suggests that the agency should (in addition to the points at 5.7 above):

- identify itself clearly, although there is no duty on the agency at this stage to disclose the identity of the employer on whose behalf it is advertising;

- make it clear in the job advert if the agency intends to pass on applicants' details to one or more of their clients;

- inform potential applicants of any use they intend to make of applications that is not self-evident, for example if the agency plans to retain applicants' details for use in connection with future vacancies.

Some general guidelines for good practice in job advertising are:

- Draft advertisements so that they provide a clear and accurate picture of the organisation's activities, the duties and level of seniority of the job, and the type of candidate the organisation is seeking.

- Make sure that advertisements do not contain any material that could be construed as sexist or racist.

- Ensure that the language used in the advertisement is specific and unambiguous.

- Refrain from specifying age limits or age-related criteria in job advertisements.

- Make sure that any job-related requirements included in an advertisement are necessary for the performance of the job, and not excessive or overstated.

- Check that any employment agency to be used is reputable and ask for a statement from the agency that they will comply with all legal provisions, including the *DPA 1998*.

- Make job applicants sourced from employment agencies aware of the employer's identity as soon as possible.

Dealing lawfully with data obtained on application forms

5.9 With the publication of the Employment Practices Code, employers would be well advised to review, and if necessary, amend their application forms if they have not already done so recently. A further beneficial course of action might be to devise different versions of the application form for use for recruitment into different types of jobs.

Job applications may be received in several ways:

- on company-designed application forms;

- in CVs written by individual job applicants;

- online applications; and

- summaries provided by recruitment agencies in the agency's style and format.

Security of job applications

5.10 Whatever method of receiving applications is chosen, the employer has a duty under the seventh data protection principle to ensure that any personal data they hold about job applicants is held securely and in such a way that it is protected against unauthorised or unlawful processing, accidental loss, or destruction or damage. The Code of Practice suggests the following measures:

- ensuring that a secure method of electronic transmission is used where applications are sought online;

- limiting access to electronic applications by ensuring they are saved in a directory or drive to which only authorised personnel have access;

- ensuring that paper applications (whether postal or faxed) are given directly to the person responsible for processing the applications, and stored under lock and key;

- if applications are processed by line managers, make sure they are aware of how they should store them.

It is also advisable to ensure that:

- applications can be accessed only by those who are actively engaged in the process of recruitment; and

- line managers who review job applications are made aware of the necessary data protection provisions in relation to job applications.

Company application forms

5.11 Whilst an employer may not have much control over the design of an individual's CV, they will be able to control the information provided by applicants on in-house application forms to a significant extent. Apart from the importance of designing application forms to ensure the collection of all the necessary information for the purpose of effective recruitment, the form should:

- identify the employer clearly, ie provide the employer's name, address and other contact details;

- advise applicants if the information they provide on the application form is to be used for any purpose other than recruitment into the post for which they are applying (for example applicants should be informed if their information may be retained for recruitment into different posts, or is likely to be passed on to another organisation);

- include a statement asking candidates to choose (perhaps by ticking a yes/no box) whether to apply for only a specific post, or to opt to have their details kept on file (in the event that they are unsuccessful in their application) in case other positions arise in the future;

- request only information that is appropriate, relevant and necessary for the job being considered – this ties in to the third data protection principle which requires employers to ensure that personal data is 'adequate, relevant and not excessive in relation to the purpose or purposes for which they are processed';

- ensure the scope of the information requested is proportionate to the employer's aim – the Guidance provides a clear example by pointing out that the extent and nature of the information required of an applicant for the post of head of security at a bank would be very different from the information required of an applicant to work in the same bank's staff canteen;

- be designed so that the applicant's personal details (ie address, gender, marital or family status, age, nationality, etc) can be separated from the remainder of the form (normally by HR department) before the application is passed through to line managers for short-listing (in order to promote equality of opportunity and the avoidance of discrimination);

- not include any questions that request information that will become relevant only if the applicant is subsequently employed (for example information about a job applicant's partner or children, which might become necessary after employment has commenced for insurance purposes, but would not be relevant to the recruitment decision);

- only ask for information about an applicant's criminal convictions if this information is necessary in relation to the post to be filled;

- make a statement on the form about any checks that the employer routinely makes at a later stage of the recruitment process in order to verify information provided by the applicant;

- ensure there is justification for seeking any sensitive data from the applicant, and if there is justification, explain the reason(s) why the information is being sought (see 5.13 below).

In order to comply with the *DPA 1998* and the Code of Practice, employers should, if they have not already arranged to do so, use more than one version of their application form and customise each version to the type of post in question. The principle behind this is to ensure that job applicants are not asked questions that are irrelevant to the post for which they are applying. Each version of the form can nevertheless contain the same core questions. Distinctions may be drawn in a number of ways, including the following examples (which are not, of course, exhaustive):

- manual and non-manual jobs (so-called 'blue collar' and 'white collar' posts);

- support staff jobs and professional jobs;

- managerial and non-managerial posts;

- office-based and travelling jobs, for example sales executives.

The aim should be to ensure that, insofar as is possible and practicable, the employer should not seek information from job applicants that is not directly relevant to the specific post for which they are applying. Examples of information that might be relevant to some jobs, but not others, could, for example, include information on whether the applicant holds a driving licence, information on criminal convictions, degree of computer literacy, etc.

It is advisable for employers to devise and implement a policy on the handling, retention and disposal of applications for employment, including unsolicited applications. The policy should include the length of time that the employer will retain application forms (see 5.32 below), the method and frequency of destroying out-of-date applications and the circumstances in which an application may be held for longer than the default period.

Online applications

5.12   The principles outlined at 5.11 above would apply equally to job applications sent online. Where this method of receiving applications is used, the employer should take steps to ensure that applications can be sent securely, for example by using encryption-based software.

Sensitive data in relation to job applications

5.13   The *DPA 1998* states that sensitive data may not be gathered about an individual unless either the person has consented to processing, or one of a restricted number of conditions is fulfilled. One of these conditions is if the data is necessary in order for the employer to comply with a legal obligation in connection with employment.

Where data is necessary to comply with a legal obligation

5.14   As stated at 5.13 above, one of the conditions justifying the collection and use of sensitive data is where the data is necessary in order for the employer to comply with a legal obligation. This can be an obligation imposed by statute or by common law (ie as a result of court and tribunal decisions that set binding precedents as to how the law should be interpreted). Thus employers that wish to seek information about job applicants' previous convictions; information about the applicant's physical or mental health; racial or ethnic origins; or religion could justify doing so if they were confident that the data was necessary in order to fulfil a legal duty.

Although there is a fairly wide scope for employers to use compliance with a legal obligation as a condition to justify the collection of sensitive data during recruitment and selection, it should be noted that the wording of the law requires the processing of sensitive data to be *necessary* for compliance with a legal obligation (ie not just desirable or convenient for the employer).

Legal reasons why it may be necessary for an employer to collect sensitive data about job applicants could include the following duties:

- to check, prior to appointment, whether a job applicant has the right to work in the UK (see 5.29 below);

- not to discriminate on the grounds of sex, trans-gender status, marital status, civil partnership status, pregnancy, sexual orientation, race, religion/belief or (unless there is justification) age or disability;

- to make reasonable adjustments under the *Disability Discrimination Act 1995* (see 5.18 below) which may justify the collection of information about a job applicant's health;

- to ensure the security of employees' and customers' personal data under the *DPA 1998* and the consequent need to ensure that applicants for posts in which personal data is handled are honest, reliable and trustworthy – this may justify collecting information about applicants' previous convictions (see 5.16 and 5.30 below);

- to ensure the health, safety and welfare of people at work, which would justify the collection of information about job applicants' health.

The above list is, of course, not exhaustive.

Gaining employees' consent to the processing of sensitive data

5.15 It is advisable for employers to design their application forms so that they contain a statement to be signed by the applicant to signify their consent to the sensitive data contained in the application form being processed by the employer. An example of such a statement could read:

'Information from this application may be processed for purposes registered by the Company under the Data Protection Act 1998. I hereby give my consent to [company name] processing the data supplied in this application form for the purpose of recruitment and selection.'

The Code of Practice points out, however, that consent to the processing of sensitive data must be 'explicit', and 'freely given'. 'Explicit' in this context is defined as meaning that the applicant must have signed a document indicating their agreement, having first been clearly informed how the information will be used. 'Freely given' is described as giving the applicant a real choice whether or not to consent to the processing, and operating a policy of not subjecting any applicant who declines to give their consent to a significant detriment.

It can be seen from the above interpretation of the phrase 'freely given' that the extent to which employers may rely on job applicants' consent to the processing of sensitive data is somewhat limited. Although individuals obviously have a free choice as to whether or not to apply for a particular job and, as part of their application, to choose whether or not to provide any sensitive data that the organisation has requested, consent to the processing of sensitive data as a condition of a job offer is less likely to fall into the category of 'freely given'.

As stated above, employers should always assess properly whether there is justification for seeking any sensitive data from job applicants, in line with the requirements of the post in question. If there is justification, the application form should clearly explain the reason(s) why the information is being sought.

Information about job applicants' criminal convictions

5.16 Information about a job applicant's criminal convictions constitutes sensitive data under the *DPA 1998*. Job applicants also have certain rights under the *Rehabilitation of Offenders Act 1974*. Under this Act, a conviction becomes 'spent' after the elapse of a defined period of time, which in turn depends on the type of conviction and the length of time that has elapsed since it occurred. Where a conviction is spent, this allows a job applicant to be treated for most purposes as if it had never happened and to decline to disclose it during the recruitment process. There are, however, a large number of jobs that are exempt from the non-disclosure principle (listed in the *Rehabilitation of Offenders Act 1974 (Exceptions) Order 1975 (SI 1975 No 1023)*).

Because the right to conceal a spent conviction is a statutory right conferred on job applicants by the *Rehabilitation of Offenders Act 1974*, it is unlawful for an employer to refuse to employ someone because they have declined to disclose a spent conviction. Equally, if a job applicant elects to disclose a spent conviction voluntarily, or if the employer happens to find out about it from another source, the employer must disregard it when making the decision as to whom to employ.

The Code of Practice recommends that employers should only ask for information about an applicant's criminal convictions if this can be justified in terms of the job in question. Questions about an applicant's criminal convictions might be necessary, for example, if the job was one covered by the *Rehabilitation of Offenders Act 1974 (Exceptions) Order 1975*, in which case the employer would be entitled to ask for all convictions (including spent convictions) to be declared in order to comply with the law in this area. Where this is the case, this fact should be clearly stated on the application form or accompanying letter. For most jobs, however, applicants would (under the provisions of the *Rehabilitation of Offenders Act 1974*) be under no obligation to disclose spent convictions and, if a question asking whether the applicant had any previous convictions was contained in the form, would be entitled to answer 'no'. Applicants are, however, – if asked – required to disclose convictions that are not spent.

The Guidance recommends that employers should not be tempted to gather information about *all* job applicants' criminal convictions, but instead should restrict any enquiries of this nature to the successful applicant only (unless there are special circumstances justifying a different approach).

Employers may also apply to the Criminal Records Bureau (CRB) or Disclosure Scotland for information about a job applicant's previous convictions. This matter is dealt with at 5.30 below.

Information gathered for monitoring purposes

5.17 Many organisations carry out monitoring of job applicants in order to promote equality of opportunity as between people of different racial groups and both sexes and protect against any inequalities that may otherwise creep into the recruitment process. Although information about an individual's racial or ethic origin is classed as sensitive data under the *DPA 1998*, it is legitimate for an employer to request this information from job applicants if the purpose of doing so is equal opportunities monitoring. Once again this purpose should be clearly stated on the application form in such a way that it is made clear that the racial background of the applicant will not in any way influence the selection decision (which would in any event be in breach of the *Race Relations Act 1976*).

Information about a job applicant's disability

5.18 Any information gathered about a job applicant's physical or mental health or condition will fall into the category of 'sensitive data'. There are, however, sound legal reasons to ask job applicants whether they have any disability on account of the employer's duty under the *Disability Discrimination Act 1995* to make 'reasonable adjustments' to working arrangements to accommodate the needs of a disabled applicant (or employee) in order to reduce the substantial disadvantage that the applicant would otherwise have in seeking employment. This subject is explored fully in CHAPTER 7.

There may also be solid grounds of requesting information about applicants' physical and mental health in order to comply with the employer's duty under the *Health and Safety at Work Act 1974* to ensure, in so far as is reasonably practicable, the health, safety and welfare of all staff at work.

71

Dealing with interview records

5.19 Keeping a record of each job applicant's interview will be an important and necessary part of the recruitment process in order for the employer to be able to objectively review and assess each candidate's suitability for the job in question. It will be especially important to keep a record of the reason(s) for the selection of the successful applicant and the reasons for the rejection of the unsuccessful candidates. The Code of Practice states in relation to interview records that the employer must be able to justify the retention of personal data created following an interview, ie that the record keeping must be relevant to and necessary for the process of recruitment and for defending the process against possible legal challenge.

The records should be objective and should focus on factors such as the extent to which a candidate's qualifications, skills and experience match up to the requirements of the job, as defined in the employee specification. Aspects of the applicant's personal background such as family circumstances should not form part of the record as this may, for example, be perceived as discriminatory against a female candidate.

The existence of clear records will be helpful also in the event that one of the unsuccessful candidates brings a claim for unlawful discrimination to an employment tribunal. The record will assist the employer to convince the tribunal that its recruitment practices were objective, that the recruitment exercise was approached in a professional manner and that the selection decision was based on the successful candidate's merit and not on personal factors such as sex, race or age. If, on the other hand, no records are kept, it will be extremely difficult for the employer to convince a tribunal that the recruitment exercise was carried out fairly and objectively, and the tribunal may conclude, in the absence of a satisfactory explanation, that the selection decision was discriminatory.

The first data protection principle states that personal data must be processed fairly and lawfully. 'Lawfully' in this context is likely to be interpreted widely. It would follow that any form of unlawful discrimination, ie unfavourable treatment of an applicant (at any stage of the recruitment process) on grounds of sex, pregnancy, marital status, civil partnership status, sexual orientation, trans-gender status, colour, race, nationality, ethic origin, national origin, religion or belief, age or disability would be likely to breach this principle.

The right of access to interview records

5.20 When making interview notes, whether on a pre-designed form or not, it should be borne in mind that the job applicant will have the right of access to this information on request (under the subject access provisions of the *DPA 1998*). The interviewer should therefore take care not to record any observations that they would be uncomfortable with the applicant reading. The best guideline is to record only observable facts, or else personal opinions that are backed up by facts. It may, for example, be acceptable to state that the job applicant was 'hesitant' when asked questions on a particular topic, but unwise to record that they would 'not fit in' as this latter observation would tend to be a highly subjective and judgmental statement (and could possibly be influenced – sometimes subconsciously – by the applicant's racial or cultural background). In general, any notes made about the applicant should be capable of being justified by facts, not feelings. So long as the interviewer focuses on the requirements of the job and the extent to which the applicant's background matches these, rather than on personal opinions and impressions of the applicant, they will not go far wrong.

Retention of interview notes

5.21   Once the recruitment process is complete, there will be no longer any good reason to retain the successful candidate's interview notes since the purpose of these will be purely to assist the employer to select the most suitable candidate for the job. The notes should therefore not be carried over into the person's permanent personnel file as it is unlikely that they can serve any further useful or legitimate purpose.

Carrying out checks on job applicants

5.22   Considerable time, effort and expense is usually involved in the process of recruitment. It is therefore entirely legitimate for the employer, prior to committing to an offer of employment, to seek to check that the information supplied by the preferred job applicant is accurate and complete and to obtain references from previous employers. It would be simplistic and foolish to assume that all job applicants always told the whole truth about their qualifications, skills and experience during the process of recruitment. Often an applicant will present information in the most favourable light, perhaps giving undue emphasis to a particular aspect of their experience, playing down a weakness or gap in their skills or even implying that a qualification has been obtained when it has not. Whilst a well-structured, thorough interview should bring these issues to light (provided good, probing questions are asked), it is nevertheless advisable to carry out certain routine checks, at least on the applicant selected as the preferred new recruit. Whilst some organisations choose to seek references on *all* job applicants, even prior to interview, this is time-consuming and arguably unnecessary.

As stated at 5.11 above, the employer should include a statement on all company application forms informing prospective job applicants of any checks that they routinely make in order to verify the information provided by the applicant. This information should be repeated at the interview, ie the candidate should be made fully aware of the types of checks that the employer intends to carry out (with the applicant's consent – see below), what information will be verified and how the checks will be carried out (including information about any external sources that will be used to carry out the checks). The employer should also inform job applicants if the successful candidate will be required to undergo a pre-employment medical examination as a condition of employment (see CHAPTER 7).

The Code of Practice and Supplementary Guidance set out a number of key principles about vetting job applicants, including recommendations that employers should:

- carry out checks only on individuals who have been selected for employment and not on all job applicants;

- only vet job applicants where there are particular and significant risks involved in the job and where there is no less intrusive way of obtaining the necessary information;

- seek to obtain relevant information directly from the job applicant and then verify it, rather than seeking information about the applicant directly from a third party;

- use vetting as a means of obtaining specific information, not as a means of gathering general intelligence (see 5.27 below);

- use all reasonable means to ensure that any external sources used as part of the vetting process are reliable.

More detailed checks, such as vetting an individual's background and personal circumstances, or vetting of their family members, would be permitted under the *DPA 1998* and the Code of Practice only where the job was one in which special circumstances or risks applied, for example jobs involving supervision of children or certain jobs in government. Even then, the Code recommends that vetting of this nature should only be carried out where:

- they are proportionate to the specific risks faced by the employer;

- they would be likely to reveal information that would be directly relevant to the decision as to whether or not to employ the individual;

- there is no alternative less intrusive way of carrying out the necessary checks on the individual; and

- it is certain that the external source to be used for vetting is a reliable source.

If it is deemed appropriate and necessary to carry out checks on the applicant's family members (for example in the case of recruitment of police officers or prison officers), the employer should bear in mind the rights of the individuals in question to be informed that information about them will be sought and the purposes for which it will be used.

Obtaining consent for carrying out checks

5.23 The Code of Practice is quite explicit in recommending that the employer should always obtain a job applicant's signed consent before seeking to conduct any checks involving the release of information from a third party. This is in line with the general principle of openness and transparency that underpins the *DPA 1998* and the Code of Practice. Employers should not be tempted to conduct 'secret' enquiries into a job applicant's background, however useful they think such enquiries might prove to be. The job applicant has a right to know what the employer's intentions are in respect of any and all checks, before the checks are instigated.

The job applicant's consent for the necessary checks can be obtained either by including an appropriate statement on the application form for the applicant to sign, although a better route would be to use a specially designed form which the applicant could be asked to sign during the course of the interview. Such a form could read:

> I hereby authorise [the company] to take up references from any or all of my previous employers and (after any offer of employment has been confirmed in writing) from my present employer. In addition, I hereby authorise [the company] to carry out checks on my qualifications as [the company] deems appropriate.

The form should, of course be signed and dated by the job applicant.

The *DPA 1998, section 56* provides that it is unlawful to make it a condition of employment that a job applicant must, in connection with recruitment, provide the employer with a record obtained elsewhere by virtue of the individual's subject access rights. This means that employers are not permitted to force job applicants to use their subject access rights under the Act to gain access to information held by other organisations, for example information about criminal convictions held on file. There are exceptions to this provision where the imposition of the requirement to provide a record is required by law or is justified as being in the public interest.

What to do if checks reveal discrepancies

5.24 Rather controversially, the Code of Practice recommends that, where any of the checks carried out on the job applicant produce inconsistencies or discrepancies, the employer should not assume automatically that the applicant has supplied incorrect or deliberately misleading information, but instead should give the applicant the opportunity to 'make representations', ie provide an explanation for the discrepancy between the information they have provided and the information revealed as a result of the check. This may be done either by writing to the applicant or by asking them to come in for a second interview.

An obvious problem with this recommendation is that the information obtained from a third party may have been given in confidence, for example in a job reference. If this is the case, the employer may nevertheless be able to address the matter satisfactorily, for example by holding a further interview and asking the job applicant questions pertinent to the area of the discrepancy without disclosing the exact content or source of the reference.

Where, on the other hand, straightforward factual information has been supplied, for example a statement from a university or college that the applicant failed to obtain a particular qualification (in circumstances where the applicant had previously intimated to the employer that they had gained the qualification in question), then the employer would normally be able to put the statement directly to the applicant and give them the opportunity to provide an explanation. This is because the information would not be confidential. No organisation is, after all, infallible and it could happen that the university or college had made a mistake in supplying the information, for example on account of a mix-up of identities. The employer should therefore remain open-minded when carrying out checks and should not be too quick to pass judgement on an applicant about whom negative information is received, but instead should explore the issue further and take a reasoned decision as to where the truth lies. When dealing with such issues, the employer should bear in mind the fourth data protection principle, ie the duty on the employer to ensure personal data are accurate and, where necessary, kept up to date.

References

5.25 A reference that contains factual information about a job applicant's past work experience and performance can usually be viewed as a sound predictor of their future performance in a similar role. It can therefore be very useful for employers to obtain references from the successful job applicant's previous employers, if the previous employers are willing to provide them. Indeed, it is sound practice to make any job offer conditional upon the receipt of references that are satisfactory to the employer. This allows the employer, in the event that one or more of the successful candidate's references prove to be unsatisfactory, to withdraw the job offer without being in breach of contract.

It should be borne in mind that, apart from the financial services industry, employers are under no legal duty to provide job references. Many employers these days have a policy of not providing references, or else of providing only the bare minimum of factual information, ie confirmation of the dates of the person's employment and their job title. Those responsible for recruitment should not, therefore, draw adverse inferences because a previous employer has declined to provide a reference.

It is advisable for each employer to draw up a policy on giving references on behalf of ex-employees and to ensure this policy is properly communicated to all those who might reasonably expect to receive reference requests. The policy should state who in the organisation is authorised to give references, distinguish between references given on behalf of the employer ('corporate references') and personal references and lay down any restrictions on what should be written in a corporate reference. Often it is appropriate to prohibit line managers or others from providing corporate references, but instead require all requests for references to be passed to the HR manager. In this way, consistency in approach will be practised and the organisation protected to a considerable degree against the likelihood of spurious claims arising from allegedly unfair or inaccurate references. Alternatively, it could be made clear in the policy that if a line manager wishes to provide a reference for an ex-employee, they may do so only in a personal capacity, ie not on company-headed notepaper and not stating the manager's job title.

Part 2 of the Employment Practices Code (Employment Records) recommends that employers should not provide confidential references about an employee unless they are sure that this is the employee's wish. It is therefore advisable for a company policy to make it clear that references will be provided only if it is known that this is in line with the employee's wishes. To facilitate adherence to the policy, it would be good practice for employers to establish, at the time an employee leaves their employment, whether or not they wish references to be provided in respect of future job applications to other employers and to record the employee's wishes on file. Alternatively, if there is any doubt at the time a reference request is received, the employer should endeavour to contact the ex-employee to check whether they are content for the employer to provide a reference.

Although employers are, as a general rule, not obliged to provide a reference for an employee who has left their employment, court and tribunal precedents indicate that if they do so, they are under a duty of care to ensure that the information they provide in the reference is factual, accurate and not misleading.

As stated earlier, employers should ensure that all applicants are clearly informed at an early stage that obtaining references will form part of the recruitment process.

References – how to handle subject access requests

5.26   The question of whether and to what extent an individual has the right of access to a job reference provided in confidence about them under the *DPA 1998* is somewhat complex and often misunderstood.

There is an exemption under the Act applicable to individuals' access to job references about them in respect of the organisation that supplied the reference. No exemption exists, however, once the reference is in the hands of the organisation to which it has been provided. In the event of the transfer of an employee from one part of an organisation to another in circumstances where the employee's 'new' department has sought and received a reference from the department where the employee originally worked, no exemption from the right of access would arise. This means that employers would be obliged under the Act to treat requests for access to internal references in the same way as access requests in relation to any other personal information, ie disclosure would normally be required.

Although a job applicant about whom confidential references have been obtained and placed in a structured recruitment file would, potentially, have the right of access to those references, a further issue is that the reference, if disclosed, would be likely to reveal the identity of a third party, namely the author of the reference. The *DPA 1998, section 7(4)–(6)* specifies that an employer is not obliged to comply with a subject access request in circumstances where doing so would reveal information relating to a third party who could be identified from the information disclosed. This exclusion includes information identifying the third party as the source (ie the author) of the information sought by the applicant. Because disclosing a reference would reveal the identity of the person who provided it and thus represent a possible breach of the duty of confidence owed to that person, this falls squarely within these provisions. The Act also states, however, that this exclusion 'does not excuse the data controller (ie the employer) from communicating so much of the information sought by the request as can be communicated without disclosing the identity of the other individual concerned, whether by the omission of names or other identifying particulars or otherwise'.

The employer should therefore consider whether it is possible to:

- photocopy the reference in such a way as to remove the name of the employer and the name of the person who signed the reference from the copy, and provide the copy to the applicant;

- seek the consent of the author of the reference for it to be disclosed to the applicant;

- consider whether it is reasonable in all the circumstances to comply with the job applicant's subject access request without the consent of the author of the reference (for example if the company in which the applicant was previously employed no longer exists and the location of the author is not known).

Clearly if the author of the reference expressly and with good reason refuses to give their consent to the disclosure of the reference to the applicant, and if it is not possible to disclose the reference without also disclosing their identity, then the reference should not be disclosed. The employer should make a file note to this effect, recording clearly the fact that they attempted to obtain consent. This would be especially important if contact with the author of the reference was made by telephone. Refusal to consent should not, however, be assumed, and the employer should take reasonable steps to try to secure the necessary consent.

The Employment Practices Code points out, however, that releasing a reference following a subject access request might not in reality be a breach of the duty of confidence owed to the third party. Often a reference will contain only factual information about an individual such as the dates of their previous employment or the number of days absence they have had. Since this information will already be known to the individual who is the subject of the reference, there will be nothing contentious or confidential in the reference and, arguably, no proper reason to refuse to disclose it.

The general principle is that references should normally be disclosed to the employee following a valid subject access request, unless the author of the reference provides some compelling reason as to why it should be edited or not released.

Social networking sites

5.27 Many people nowadays choose to use social networking sites and some may choose to disclose a great deal of personal information about themselves on the site. Some of this information might be of interest to an employer for the purpose of selecting new employees. It is relatively easy to look up a particular individual on a social networking site and to learn much about their private life. Even though the individual will have chosen freely to disclose that information on the site and it is therefore (arguably) in the public domain, that does not mean that the employer can necessarily use it for the purpose of deciding whom to appoint. Indeed routinely researching information about job applicants via social networking sites is widely considered to be contrary to good practice.

Where employers carry out equal opportunities monitoring during the recruitment process, this is generally done by asking candidates to disclose personal information about themselves (such as marital status, age, ethnic origins, religion etc) on a separate, tear-off portion of the application form so that this personal information is not used when the employer decides whom to select. A practice of checking individuals' online profiles as part of the application process would turn the monitoring exercise into a travesty because the personal information obtained from the social networking site would not be part of the separate monitoring process but would instead become one of the criteria on which selection was based. For example, an individual may have disclosed information on a social networking site that indicates they hold to a particular religious belief, but employers are not permitted (except in very limited circumstances) to take an individual's religion into account when deciding whom to recruit. Employers should not, therefore, routinely research information about job applicants on social networking sites.

Quite apart from the above considerations, obtaining information about an individual in this way without the individual's consent would be in breach of the DPA. This is because the DPA requires employers to inform employees or job applicants about any type of monitoring that they intend to carry out (in advance of doing so) and such monitoring must be proportionate to the employer's legitimate business needs. CHAPTER 9 discusses the subject of monitoring in depth whilst CHAPTER 8 discusses equality and equal opportunities monitoring.

Checks on qualifications

5.28   Where it is necessary for an employee to hold a particular qualification in order to be able to perform the job effectively, the employer should always check that the successful job applicant's qualifications have actually been obtained. This can most readily be done by requesting sight of the original of the appropriate certificates and retaining a copy of these on file. Ideally, this check should be done before any job offer is made. If not, the offer letter should state that the production of documentary evidence about the applicant's qualifications is a pre-condition for employment.

If the employer wishes to verify further that the applicant has the requisite qualifications for the job by writing to the university or college where the qualification was obtained, this should be done only with the employee's express consent. Some universities and colleges may in any event require a signed approval form from the individual before they will release confirmation of their qualifications to a third party.

Checks on applicants' right to work in the UK

5.29 Under the *Immigration, Asylum and Nationality Act 2006*, it is a criminal offence for an employer to recruit someone who:

- has not been granted leave to enter or remain in the UK; or

- does not have permission to work in the UK.

Employers therefore have duty under the *Immigration, Asylum and Nationality Act 2006* to check that anyone who is subject to immigration control and whom they wish to employ has the right to work in the UK. The Act does not apply to the employment of British citizens; Commonwealth citizens with the right of abode in the UK; citizens of any country in the European Economic Area; and citizens of Switzerland.

To fulfil their duty under the *Immigration, Asylum and Nationality Act 2006*, employers should take the following steps to check whether the applicant has the right to work in the UK:

- require the job applicant to produce either one or two original documents in defined combinations, indicating that they have the right to work in the UK;

- check that the documents appear to relate to the job applicant; and

- either retain the documents or keep a copy of them for the duration of the person's employment and for two years after termination of employment.

There are heavy fines for employing illegal migrants and doing so knowingly is a criminal offence. Appropriate checks must be carried out satisfactorily before the applicant is permitted to start work. Employers are expected to take reasonable steps to verify the authenticity of any documents produced by job applicants for this purpose, although they are not expected to be experts in this area. Employers should, however take the following steps:

- check any photographs on documents to make sure they are consistent with the job applicant's appearance;

- check the date of birth on the documents to ensure consistency with the job applicant's appearance;

- if any document contains a different name from the one used in the person's application, request further documentation to explain the reason for the discrepancy (eg a marriage certificate); and

- check the expiry dates of any leave for the individual to enter or remain in the UK and any endorsements in the passport.

Employers should take care, when approaching the matter of a job applicant's right to work in the UK that they do not engage in practices that could amount to race discrimination. The *Race Relations Act 1976* requires employers not to treat any job applicant unfavourably on the grounds of nationality. Reconciling the requirements of the *Race Relations Act 1976* with the requirements of the *Immigration, Asylum and Nationality Act 2006* can be a challenge. Help is at hand in the form of a Code of Practice on the avoidance of race discrimination in recruitment, available from the UK Border Agency at: www.ukba.homeoffice.gov.uk. The main recommendation of this Code of Practice is that employers, in carrying out checks of job applicants' right to work in the UK, should require *all* applicants (and not only those who are known or believed to be of foreign nationality) to produce documentary evidence of their right to work in the UK.

One effective way of dealing with this matter sensibly is to include a statement within all letters sent out inviting job applicants to interview to the effect that the employer will require documentary evidence of the right to work in the UK. This can be conveniently combined with a request to bring proof of qualifications to the interview. It is advisable also to inform applicants that it is the organisation's policy to make such a request, and that all job applicants are required to comply. At the interview itself, the interviewer can request sight of the relevant documents, and make copies for the company's retention.

Checks on criminal records

5.30 Employers may apply to the Criminal Records Bureau (CRB) for information about a job applicant's previous convictions. Such applications must be made in association with the job applicant and must be in relation to a specific post. Applications will be accepted only where the employer is registered with the CRB. In Scotland, applications may be made to Disclosure Scotland.

There are three types of certificate, although at the time of writing only the first two are available in England (all three are available in Scotland):

- A criminal records certificate (CRC), which is issued jointly to the individual and a registered employer and includes information on both spent and unspent convictions. This is known as a standard disclosure and the certificate is available in relation to recruitment into posts that are exempt from the provisions of the *Rehabilitation of Offenders Act 1974*.

- An enhanced criminal records certificate (ECRC), which is available jointly to the individual and a registered employer and which includes more detailed information than the CRC. This is known as an enhanced disclosure and the certificate would be appropriate where, for example, the work involved unsupervised contact with children or vulnerable adults.

- A criminal conviction certificate (CCC) which will eventually be available to individual applicants in England and will show unspent convictions only. This is known as a basic disclosure. Once these are available employers will be able to ask job applicants to produce a CCC if they wish at an appropriate point in the recruitment process.

All information about individuals obtained from the CRB or Disclosure Scotland will fall into the category of sensitive data and must be treated accordingly.

Employers should, as a first step, review whether it is objectively necessary to request a disclosure from the CRB or Disclosure Scotland in relation to each individual post, bearing in mind the third data protection principle (ie that information must be adequate, relevant and not excessive in relation to the purpose for which it is processed). The Code of Practice recommends that employers should:

- not routinely ask all short-listed applicants to obtain a disclosure from the CRB or Disclosure Scotland but confine requests for disclosures to those whom the employer intends to appoint;

- keep any information obtained from the CRB or Disclosure Scotland confidential and not share it with other employers; and

- not seek information about criminal convictions by forcing an applicant to use their subject access rights from sources other than the CRB or Disclosure Scotland.

The Guidance points out that seeking to obtain information about a job applicant's spent convictions from old newspaper articles or similar media sources for a post that is not eligible for standard or enhanced disclosure is likely to be in breach of the DPA.

Employees' rights in relation to automated decisions in recruitment

5.31 The *DPA 1998, section 12* contains specific provisions relating to certain forms of decision-making carried out solely by automated means. Examples include circumstances in which the automated decision-making process evaluates matters such as job applicants' work performance, creditworthiness, reliability or conduct.

Job applicants' rights in this case are to be informed that a decision about them has been taken on the basis of an automated decision-taking process, and to challenge the automated decision if, as a result of it, they have been rejected for employment or treated significantly differently from other applicants. The applicant's challenge must be made in writing within 21 days of the employer informing him or her of the automated decision. The applicant would have the right to request an explanation of the logic involved in the decision, and to ask for the decision to be reconsidered or retaken on a different basis, ie not solely on the basis of the automatic processing. The employer is obliged to provide a response within 21 days. These rights only apply, however, where the employer's decision has been taken *solely* by automated means and not in circumstances where the rejection of a particular job applicant was as a result of a range of factors, at least some of which involved human intervention or analysis.

These provisions mean that job applicants can, in certain circumstances, challenge decisions about their suitability for a job made on the basis of psychometric testing carried out and analysed by means of a computer-based software.

The Code of Practice recommends that employers should be certain that any psychometric testing that they employ for the purpose of short-listing or final selection is done only by people who are qualified to apply and assess the particular test. This is, in any event, common sense and essential good practice and is consistent with the third data protection principle which requires employers to ensure that personal data are adequate in relation to the purpose for which they are used.

In light of these provisions, employers should:

- ensure that any psychometric tests to be used have been fully validated;

- review whether any tests used within the organisation measure factors that are relevant to the post in question;

- ensure that any psychometric tests to be used are applied and assessed only by people who have been fully trained in their use;

- set up a system that ensures job applicants are informed up-front if an automated system is to be used as the sole basis of short-listing and how they can challenge any decision made in this way that results in their rejection;

- keep the results of any automated testing under regular review to ensure the tests achieve the outcomes that the employer seeks and that they treat applicants fairly;

- put a system in place to deal with any challenges raised by job applicants following the results of any testing conducted by auto-mated means; and

- refrain from using automated testing as the sole means of short-listing.

Deciding for how long recruitment records should be retained

5.32   There is no time period prescribed in the *DPA 1998* or the Code of Practice in relation to the retention of recruitment records. Employers are therefore free to decide what time period is appropriate for their business needs. Employers should, however, bear the fifth data protection principle in mind – that records should not be kept for longer than is necessary in relation to the purpose for which they were created.

The time limit for a job applicant to bring a claim of discrimination to an employment tribunal is three months after the alleged act of discrimination (usually the date the rejection letter was received). Employers should therefore keep recruitment records for between four and six months (which allows a safety window), after which they should be destroyed. Clearly, however, if a claim for discrimination is lodged with the employment tribunal, then the employer would be justified in retaining the files of the claimant and possibly those of the other short-listed candidates for a longer period, ie until the discrimination claim had been settled. This would be in order to be able to prove to the tribunal's satisfaction that the applicant claiming discrimination was not in fact treated less favourably than other applicants.

As stated in 5.29 above, documents obtained for the purpose of proving a job applicant's right to work in the UK must, by law, be retained throughout employment and then for two years after termination of employment.

The Code of Practice also recommends that employers should:

- assess who in the organisation retains recruitment records;

- establish a policy on a suitable retention period for recruitment records based on clear business needs, ensuring that no recruitment records are held beyond the statutory period in which a claim can be brought to court or tribunal;

- adhere to that policy unless there are special reasons to retain a particular record for a longer period, for example if there is an ongoing legal claim against the employer from a particular job applicant;

- destroy information obtained as a result of any vetting exercise as soon as possible, and in any event within six months, although the Code suggests a record of the result of vetting or verification may be retained, ie a simple record of whether the result was satisfactory or unsatisfactory;

- destroy information about an individual's criminal convictions once these have been verified through the CRB or Disclosure Scotland, unless there are exceptional circumstances that justify retaining the information in respect of the successful applicant (ie it is necessary to retain the information for a purpose relevant to the ongoing employment relationship);

- advise unsuccessful applicants if the employer intends to retain their details on file in respect of future vacancies (rather than assuming that this would be their choice) and give them the option to ask for their details to be removed from the file, if they wish;

- ensure that all information obtained during the course of the recruitment exercise is securely stored, or else destroyed.

In relation to the destruction of information that is no longer relevant and necessary for the employer's legitimate business interests, the Guidance recommends shredding manual records and ensuring that electronic files are permanently deleted from the employer's computer system.

Chapter 6   Employee records

Introduction

6.1   The creation and maintenance of employee records will form the foundation of effective people management in all organisations, whether public or private, large or small. If the records are structured, well-organised and include information that is appropriate and relevant to the employer's needs, they will serve the employer well. If, on the other hand, records are random, unstructured or poorly organised, this will in all likelihood lead to confusion and time-wasting both in relation to subject access requests under the *Data Protection Act 1998* (*DPA 1998* or 'the Act') and in the event of any kind of claim against the employer in an employment tribunal.

Observing the data protection principles in the maintenance of employee records

6.2   The eight data protection principles contained in the Act (see CHAPTER 2) underpin an employer's duties and obligations under the Act. The Act places responsibilities on all employers to process personal data in a fair and proper way.

The first data protection principle creates the obligation on employers to process personal data 'fairly and lawfully'. This duty is subject to the proviso that personal data must not be processed unless one of a number of conditions is fulfilled. The conditions are that:

- the employee has given their consent to the processing; or

- the processing of personal data is necessary for one of the following reasons:

    - for the performance of a contract;

    - in order to ensure compliance with a legal obligation;

    - to protect the vital interests of the employee;

    - for the administration of justice or for the exercise of any public functions;

    - for the purposes of legitimate interests pursued by the employer, for example if the business was about to be transferred.

Further conditions are imposed on the processing of data that is classed as 'sensitive data' under the Act (see 4.5 above).

From the above list, the most likely valid reasons for an employer to process personal data in employment records would be:

- for the purpose of performing a contract, for example the employer may need to hold information about the employee's dependents in order to be able to process any claim for benefit under a contractual private medical insurance scheme;

- in order to ensure compliance with a legal obligation, for example to comply with the duty to process Statutory Maternity Pay for an employee who is pregnant;

- where the employee has given their consent to the processing.

It is important, however, to take note of the word 'necessary' used in this part of the Act. Unless the employee's consent has been obtained, the processing of data about them will be fair and lawful only if one of the relevant conditions is *necessary* for the business, and not just because (for example) management would find it helpful or convenient to process personal data.

The second data protection principle requires employers to obtain and use information about individuals only for one or more specified and lawful purposes and not process the information for any purpose that is incompatible with the stated purpose(s). It follows that the employer should firstly be clear as to the (lawful) purpose(s) to be served by the collection and retention of personal information about their employees. Once this is established, the employer must not subsequently use any of the information they hold on file for any purpose that is incompatible with or vastly different from the purpose for which it was collected.

An example of non-compliance in this area would be where the employer carried out monitoring of employees' use of email for the purpose of preventing and detecting unauthorised use of the employer's computer system, and as a result of such monitoring discovered by chance that the employee had disclosed in an email to a company doctor that they had developed an illness. If the employer used that information for any other purpose, for example, to deny the employee a promotion, that would be an unlawful use of the information and would almost certainly amount to a breach of trust and confidence as well.

The third data protection principle states that personal information must be adequate, relevant and not excessive in relation to the purpose or purposes for which it is processed. The employer should therefore review carefully all the information they collect and hold about employees and job applicants and check whether it is:

- sufficient to meet their needs;

- not excessive when viewed in relation to their needs; and

- relevant to the achievement of a legitimate aim.

Any policy or practice as a result of which employees are asked or expected to provide information that is not strictly appropriate, relevant and necessary to the employer's needs should be amended accordingly.

The fourth data protection principle obliges employers to ensure personal data is accurate and kept up to date. This essentially means that the employer should take all reasonable steps to ensure the accuracy of the information they hold, recognising that employees will sometimes neglect to provide up-to-date information to their employer about changes in their circumstances. This topic is dealt with at 6.6 below.

The fifth data protection principle places a duty on employers not to keep personal data for longer than is necessary in relation to the purpose(s) for which it was obtained. Neither the *DPA 1998* nor the Employment Practices Code (Employment Records) (see 6.4 below) prescribes any general time limitation on the retention of personal data. It is therefore up to each employer to decide for themselves what time periods are appropriate in relation to the needs of their business.

The sixth data protection principle requires employers to process data in accordance with individuals' rights under the *DPA 1998*. This would include the duty on the employer to ensure that subject access requests are treated properly and in accordance with the provisions of the Act (see 4.18 above).

The seventh data protection principle requires employers to put in place proper measures, eg security measures, to protect personal data against unauthorised or unlawful processing, accidental loss or destruction, or damage. This will include adequate protection for computer systems, eg proper use of passwords and possibly the use of encryption and establishment of firewalls (see 6.8 below).

The eighth data protection principle places the responsibility on employers not to transfer personal data outside the European Economic Area unless the country or territory to which it is transferred has in place an adequate level of protection for individuals' rights and freedoms in relation to the processing of personal data.

Checking up on records held by line managers

6.3 It will be up to each employer to formulate and apply a policy on employment records that sets out what records will be held about employees and other workers, the format in which they will be held and who will be responsible for holding them. Some organisations specify that only the HR department is authorised to hold records about employees, and that no line manager or other person will be entitled to retain separate records.

A blanket ban on the holding of personal records by line managers may, however, be unrealistic. For example, it may fall to a line manager to speak to an employee about a matter of minor misconduct or shortfall in performance, in which case the manager will wish to keep, at the very least, a diary note of the fact that an informal meeting took place, what was discussed, the time and date of the meeting and any outcome. It may be unwieldy or undesirable to expect line managers on every occasion to create a formal record and pass it on to the HR department for inclusion in the employee's personal file. This does not mean that this approach should be ruled out, as it would have the obvious advantage of ensuring that all records were held centrally and thus under the control of one department where they could potentially be managed more consistently, efficiently and securely. What it does mean is that each employer should review their needs and devise a policy that suits them, then ensure that the policy is applied consistently throughout the organisation. If, on the other hand, line managers are to retain their own files about employees, the employer should ensure that proper security measures are in place for the files and that line managers fully understand their responsibilities under the Act (see 6.9 below).

The starting point for an employer in relation to the management of employee records would thus be to establish a policy on these matters. At the same time it would be necessary to conduct an exercise to establish what personal information about employees existed other than in the HR department and determine whether the retention of this information was to be allowed to continue or whether the information should be assimilated into one centralised personnel records filing system.

The Code of Practice on Employment Records

6.4 The Employment Practices Code, Part 2 (Employment Records) deals specifically with employment records and provides the Information Commissioner's interpretation and recommendations as to what employers need to do to comply with the Act. The Code, like other Codes of Practice, is not legally binding on employers, but any employer who chooses not to comply with the provisions it contains is likely to find that this fact will act to their detriment in the event of a legal claim against the employer in a court or tribunal. This is because courts and tribunals will take the provisions of statutory codes of practice into account when judging such claims. It is therefore in employers' interests to pay heed to the recommendations contained in the Code and the Supplementary Guidance.

The Code of Practice does not in any way prevent an employer from collecting, maintaining or using records about their employees. Its aim is to strike a balance between an employee's right to respect for their private life and the employer's legitimate business needs, including the need to keep records for a number of reasons associated with employment. Adherence to the Code will assist employers to achieve good practice in the maintenance of records as well as helping to ensure compliance with the Act.

The Code of Practice sets down a number of general 'benchmarks' which form the foundation of its recommendations on good practice in the maintenance of employment records. These can be summarised as follows:

- The employer should nominate a senior person within the organisation to hold responsibility for ensuring on an ongoing basis that the employer's policies, procedures and practices comply with the Act. This person should have in place an established mechanism for auditing procedures in order to check that they are being followed in practice and for updating them when necessary.

- The employer should take steps to make sure that line managers who keep personal data about employees are fully conversant with their duties and responsibilities under the Act (see 6.9 below).

- Steps should also be taken to ensure all employees are made aware that they may be held personally criminally liable if they knowingly or recklessly disclose personal information without the authority to do so. In this context, the employer should, if necessary, amend any disciplinary procedures to include any breach of data protection legislation as a disciplinary offence.

- Consultation with trade unions or workers' representatives should be carried out over the design and implementation of any and all employment procedures and practices that involve the processing of personal data about employees. Although there is, at present, no legal requirement to consult in this context, it is considered good practice to do so and consultation is likely to lead to better employee relations.

- The employer should conduct an exercise to establish what personal information about employees exists within the organisation, where information is held and who is responsible for it.

- The employer should identify and remove any information held about employees which is unnecessary or irrelevant to the employment relationship, or excessive when viewed against the purpose for which it was collected. An example given in the Code of Practice of information that is unlikely to be necessary is the collection of facts about employees' personal lives outside of work. Such information, the Code suggests, should not be processed other than in circumstances where it is necessary for legal reasons, for example to ensure compliance with the maximum working hours provisions in the *Working Time Regulations 1998 (SI 1998 No 1833)*. The employer

91

should therefore critically review all the data they hold about individuals and determine whether any of it should be deleted or not collected in the first place. Although this could amount to a substantial piece of work the first time it is done, it should not prove too unwieldy if it is carried out on a regular basis.

- Before any sensitive data about employees is collected, the employer should review whether one of the conditions for processing sensitive data has been satisfied (see 4.6 above).

These general benchmarks are supplemented by further benchmarks in relation to issues such as security of records, references, sickness and accident records, equal opportunities monitoring (see CHAPTER 8), discipline, grievance and dismissal records, access requests, etc.

Collecting and keeping employee records

6.5 As part of their policy on employment records, each employer will have to decide what information to collect about their employees, in particular new employees and how they intend to ensure the accuracy of the information and keep it up to date.

There is no legal obligation to obtain employees' consent before collecting information about employees, or prospective employees, although if any sensitive data is to be sought, the employer will need to ensure that either one of the conditions for processing sensitive data is satisfied, or that they have obtained the employee's explicit consent (see 6.7 below). Despite the absence of a duty to obtain employees' consent before a record about them is set up, the employer is under a duty to inform the employee that the record exists.

The following checklist may assist employers to set up and manage their personnel records:

- The employer should, as a matter of routine, inform all new staff what records about them are to be held, the source(s) of any information held about them, the purpose for which the records are to be held, how the information will be used and who it will be disclosed to. This may be done in a number of different ways, for example by distributing a fact sheet, directing the employee to the company's intranet (and requiring them to click confirmation that they have read and understood the information provided) and/or simply including the information as part of a face-to-face induction programme.

- The employer should also make sure that they fully inform all staff, including new employees, of their rights under the Act, including their right to request access to all data held about them (see 6.14 below). For existing staff, reminders should be issued at pre-defined intervals.

• It will be important to ensure that the employer collects information about employees only when the information is necessary for the achievement of a particular business aim, and that the information gathered is relevant to the achievement of that aim. The employer can assist this process by reviewing any forms or other means used within the organisation to gather data about employees and critically evaluating whether the questions asked produce information that the employer actually needs for a legitimate purpose. If any of the forms in use contain questions that might produce information that is irrelevant or excessive when considered in light of the employer's business needs, they should be amended.

Keeping records up to date

6.6 Under the fourth data protection principle, employers are obliged to ensure personal records are accurate and kept up to date. The most effective way of achieving this is for the employer to provide each employee, on an annual basis, with a copy of all the personal information held about them that may be subject to change, and ask them to check the data for accuracy and notify any changes that are needed to bring the information up to date.

An alternative to providing a copy of the information for this purpose would be to make access to the data available online, provided the employer's computer system is set up to allow this and provided the employee has ready access to a computer. The employer would have to take steps to ensure the security of personal data put online for this purpose, ie to put measures in place that would effectively prevent employees from accessing the personal data of others.

If neither of these two options is possible or practicable, the employer will have to devise an alternative system for ensuring that their personnel records are kept up to date, as leaving this matter to chance will be likely to lead to a breach of the fourth data protection principle. It may be possible for computer systems to be set to flag up certain items held on file at pre-defined intervals either for the individual to check or so that a nomi-nated person (for example an HR officer) can speak to individuals (perhaps by telephone) to double-check whether certain data held on their file is still accurate.

Another course of action that will help to ensure accuracy in employment records is to incorporate an audit trail into computerised personnel sys-tems. In this way, a record of anyone who has created, altered or deleted a record and the date and time that the record was amended will be maintained automatically. This would enable the employer to trace the source of all changes made to data and potentially detect any errors or inaccuracies.

Dealing with sensitive data

6.7 The *DPA 1998, section 2* sets out a list of personal information which is to be regarded as 'sensitive data'. The list includes the following features of an individual:

- racial or ethnic origin;
- political opinions;
- religious beliefs or other similar beliefs;
- membership of a trade union;
- physical or mental health or condition;
- sexual life;
- the commission or alleged omission of any offence; and
- anything related to any proceedings for an offence committed or alleged to have been committed.

The *DPA 1998, Schedule 3* sets out a series of conditions, at least one of which must be met before an employer can lawfully process sensitive data about an individual. The conditions that are potentially relevant to data protection in employment are:

- where processing is necessary in order for the employer to comply with a legal obligation in connection with employment;
- where the information has been made public as a result of steps taken by the employee;
- where processing is necessary in connection with any legal proceedings, including the defence of a legal claim against the employer;
- where processing is necessary for the exercise of any functions conferred under an enactment or any functions of the Crown, a Minister of the Crown or a government department;
- where processing is necessary for medical purposes and is undertaken by a health professional or someone with an equivalent duty of confidentiality (see CHAPTER 7);
- where processing of information about individuals' racial or ethnic origin, religious beliefs or physical or mental health is for the purpose of carrying out equal opportunities monitoring (see CHAPTER 8); and

- if the employee has given their explicit consent to the processing of sensitive data about them.

This topic is explored more fully at 4.5–4.7 above.

Security of employment records

6.8 It is a legal requirement under the *DPA 1998* for the employer to protect both manual and computer-based employment records from unauthorised access, tampering and disclosure. This is because the seventh data protection principle obliges all employers to take appropriate technical and organisational measures against unauthorised or unlawful processing of personal data.

There is a limited number of exceptions to the non-disclosure principle, for example if there is a legal requirement to make the disclosure. These are explained at 4.11 above. In the event of a legal obligation to disclose personal data, the employer will still be under a duty to inform the employee that the disclosure has been made. The only exception to this will be if informing the employee of the disclosure would be likely to prejudice the prevention or detection of a crime.

Where an employer chooses to use an outside company or agency to process their data (for example by outsourcing the payroll function), there is a duty to ensure that the company or agency selected to fulfil this function has provided sufficient guarantees in respect of security measures and to check that these measures are consistently observed.

Recruitment and training of staff who have access to employment records

6.9 In order to meet its obligation under the seventh data protection principle, the employer will need to put a number of measures in place, the first of which will be to ensure that all staff who have access to employees' records as part of their jobs are reliable and competent.

It may be prudent therefore, when recruiting new staff into jobs that involve access to employment records, to conduct careful reference checks on shortlisted applicants plus a check to establish whether the individual selected for employment has any relevant past criminal convictions. The subject of carrying out checks in recruitment and selection is dealt with fully at 5.22 above.

Once recruited, the new employee will need full training in order to make sure they understand their responsibilities and duties under the Act, including the duty to keep personal data confidential, not to obtain it unlawfully, nor to disclose it to any unauthorised person. The training should also make staff aware that they can be held personally criminally liable for any breaches of the Act. A further sensible precaution to ensure security is to place confidentiality and security clauses into the employment contracts of all new staff whose jobs will take them into contact with confidential data.

It may also be advisable to inform employees who use computers in the course of their work that, under the *Computer Misuse Act 1990*, it is a criminal offence to secure unauthorised access to a computer system or to computer material in certain circumstances, or to modify the contents of a computer system without authority. 'Unauthorised modification' of computer material includes deliberate erasure or corruption of programmes or data, modifying or destroying a system file or another user's file or the addition of any programme or data to the computer's contents. It is also an offence under the *Computer Misuse Act 1990* to spread a computer virus. Although this Act applies mainly to unauthorised access to computers from external sources, it has potential application internally as well.

'Unauthorised access' for the purposes of the Act is defined as:

> 'access of any kind by a person to any programme or data held on a computer when such a person is not him or herself entitled to control access to the programme or the data and does not have consent from any person who is so entitled.'

Measures to ensure the security of employment records

6.10 In relation to the physical security of employment records, employers should undertake the following steps:

- Decide who in the organisation needs to have access to personal data held about employees and who is to have the authority to amend the data, then draw up specific guidelines to ensure that these employees understand their duties and responsibilities with regard to the confidentiality of personal data. Access to personal data should essentially be based on the needs of the employee's job, not on the seniority of the employee. Thus, direct access to employee records should not automatically be granted to managers, just because they are managers. The employer should review the needs of each person's job, make objective decisions as to who should have direct access and, if necessary, withdraw the automatic right of access to employee records from anyone for whom it is not strictly necessary. An alternative to granting line managers direct access to data about their staff is to make the data available via the HR department.

- Spell out the particular responsibilities of all employees who have access to personal data clearly and specifically, in particular those employed in the organisation's HR department or IT department.

- Design and implement a rigorous system of employee passwords (see 6.13 below).

- Ensure cabinets that contain manual records have secure locks and that a system is in place requiring them to be kept locked at all times except when in use. Keys should be held securely only by a limited number of authorised people. The aim should be to ensure that staff access employment records only when they have a legitimate business reason for doing so.

- Consult IT specialists with regard to computer security measures. It may also be useful to use the audit trail capabilities of the computer system to track who accesses and amends employment records. The audit trail can be used to follow up on any unusual pattern, for example an instance of an employee accessing someone's file noticeably more frequently than others for no obvious reason.

- Put in place rules about taking employment records outside the organisation, eg on laptop computers, and make sure this is rigorously controlled. If the employer prefers to institute a rule that bans the removal of personal data from the workplace, it may be helpful to disconnect the external disk drives from all workplace personal computers in order to physically prevent the information being transferred to laptops or other electronic devices.

- If it is permitted for certain employees to load employee records on to laptops, palmtops or blackberries (which is not recommended), put in place strict rules for the security of the devices, for example by imposing a rule that they must not be left in parked vehicles and not left unattended in the home whilst switched on.

- If information about employees has to be communicated by email, institute a system for ensuring permanent deletion of the emails from the relevant computers – and from servers – once the matter requiring communication of the data has been dealt with.

Rules and procedures on confidentiality

6.11 It is strongly advisable for employers to devise and implement clear procedures and rules governing the use of all confidential information, including data held about their employees. A company procedure on confidentiality should establish basic guidelines for employees and identify any prohibited practices so that a framework is established within which all employees can work. There should be internal controls to limit access to confidential information and to prevent the disclosure of sensitive data. The introduction and implementation of such a procedure will minimise the risks to the employer of breaches of confidentiality whilst at the same time educating employees about their individual responsibilities. This will be particularly important for employees who have access to personal data as part of their jobs. The particular responsibilities of such employees, for example those employed in the HR department or IT department, will have to be spelled out unambiguously. The rules and procedures should be made applicable to all staff, including managers, irrespective of their seniority.

Rules and procedures governing confidentiality have a number of key advantages. They:

- will clarify what information is to be treated as confidential;

- will help employees to understand their obligations;

- can define employees' key responsibilities with regard to confidential information and specify rules as to how key information should be kept confidential (eg by keeping passwords secret, etc);

- will reduce the risk of a breach of confidentiality occurring; and

- will allow the employer to enforce the rules on confidential information in the event of a breach by an employee.

Rules should cover issues such as:

- the avoidance of email, fax or text as methods of sending confidential or personal information;

- the encryption of confidential information which is to be transmitted by email;

- a ban on information being transmitted by email to and from employees' homes, unless express permission is first obtained;

- the protection of computer data when the computer is logged on, ie a rule that workstations should not be left unattended; and

- the choosing, changing and non-disclosure of passwords.

Another measure that the employer should consider in light of the duty to ensure the security of employment records is to include an express confidentiality clause in the contracts of employment of all staff who have access to confidential or personal information. The precise wording of a confidentiality clause will depend on the nature of the employer's business and the employee's position. At the very least, however, the following issues should be covered:

- the type of information that is to be regarded as confidential;

- rules on confidentiality applicable to the employee during their employment;

- rules on keeping information confidential that will apply after the termination of the employee's employment.

A sample confidentiality clause might read as follows:

'You must not at any time, other than in the proper performance of your duties, access, disclose or misuse any information that is confidential. This duty applies to you throughout your employment and following the termination of your employment. Confidential information includes any information of the Company or any of its workers, customers, suppliers or agents which the Company treats as confidential and which is not part of your own general skill and knowledge. In particular you must not disclose any information held by the Company about any of its employees or other workers to which you may have access as part of your job. Such information is to be regarded as confidential whether it is recorded in paper format, on microfiche, on computer or on disk or tape.'

Taking disciplinary action against staff who breach the employer's rules on confidentiality or security

6.12 Employers should ensure that their disciplinary procedures link in with any rules on confidentiality and that they reflect the importance of treating employment records as confidential. Disciplinary rules and procedures should make it clear that any breach of confidentiality, for example the unauthorised disclosure of personal information or careless handling of personal data, is to be regarded as a disciplinary offence which may, depending on the level of seriousness, lead to a warning or to dismissal.

One example of a case in which an employee was (fairly) dismissed for unlawful access to information held on computer was the case of *Denco Ltd v Joinson EAT* [1991] ICR 172. The employee had authority to gain access to certain files held on his employer's computer system, but was debarred from accessing other parts of the computer system. However, having learned the password for access to another part of the computer system from his daughter who worked for the same firm, he deliberately used it to gain access knowing that he was not entitled to see the sensitive information that was held there. When his activities were discovered, he was summarily dismissed, even though his motive for accessing the data was one of curiosity and not malice. The EAT held that the dismissal was fair in all the circumstances and accepted that conduct involving deliberate access to computer data without authority amounted to gross misconduct justifying summary dismissal. The EAT also commented, however, that employers should take appropriate steps to make it clear to employees that any unauthorised access to information held on computer will be regarded as gross misconduct.

It is therefore very important for employers to have clear policies governing who is, and who is not, authorised to gain access to computer data or to modify the contents of files.

Using passwords to protect employment records

6.13 One of the simplest and cheapest methods of ensuring the protection of personal data is for the employer to implement a rigorous system of employee passwords. Rules should be devised for employees governing the choosing of a password and for the regular changing of passwords. There should also be a clear written rule forbidding the disclosure of passwords to any unauthorised person, and this rule should be consistently enforced.

Specifically, the employer should enforce rules that:

- passwords must not be disclosed to any person unless written authority is first obtained from the employee's line manager;

- passwords must be changed at least every [two weeks, four weeks, six weeks] and more often if necessary;

- passwords chosen must not be obvious, for example the name of a partner, house, dog or the word 'password' or 'welcome', etc;

- any unauthorised disclosure of a password will be regarded as a disciplinary offence, rendering the employee liable to disciplinary action.

A model clause governing the use of passwords could read as follows:

'Passwords must be kept confidential at all times and should not be disclosed to anyone else unless prior written authority to do so is obtained from the relevant line manager. The line manager should be notified immediately if there is a suspicion that an employee is using a colleague's password. As a further precaution, employees should change their passwords regularly and no less frequently than once a month. Passwords should not be words or phrases that could be guessed by another person.'

Policies on handling access requests

6.14 The *DPA 1998* gives employees important rights of access to any personal information held about them by their employer. The Act expressly gives individuals the right to submit a written 'subject access request' to their employer, with which the employer must comply within 40 calendar days. Requests for access may be made in respect of manual files, micro-fiche records, audio or video tapes, computer files and email correspond-ence that contains information about the individual. The individual making the subject access request is not obliged under the Act to give any reason for seeking the information.

As a result of these provisions, employees have the right to see documents such as:

- performance reviews or appraisals;

- sickness records;

- warnings or minutes of disciplinary interviews;

- training records;

- statements about pay;

- emails or word-processed documents of which they are the subject; and

- expressions of opinion about (for example) promotion prospects (but not definite plans to promote the worker as this would fall under the 'management planning' exemption (see 4.20 above).

Employees may also request access to information generated by computer systems involving automated decision making on matters such as perform-ance and conduct.

It is a sound idea for all employers to devise a policy on the handling of subject access requests. The matters that should be incorporated into such a policy would include:

- who in the organisation is to be responsible for ensuring subject access requests are dealt with competently and promptly;

- a system for verifying the identity of anyone requesting access to their personal file, ie to ensure that personal information is disclosed only to the person who is its subject;

- to whom employees should submit subject access requests and the format in which they should make the request – guidelines should be provided, for example requesting employees to specify as precisely as possible the information to which they are seeking access;

- whether or not the employer will charge a fee for access (up to £10 per access request may be charged) or whether the £10 fee would be applied only in certain defined circumstances, for example an employer might grant one free access to each employee each year, but charge a fee for any and all further access requests during the same year; and

- a checklist that details the locations where personal data is held.

There are some limited exemptions to the general duty on employers to comply with a subject access request. These include circumstances where the information held relates to:

- management planning or forecasting;

- negotiations with employees;

- the price of a company's shares;

- the prevention or detection of crime or the apprehension or prosecution of offenders;

- the assessment or collection of any tax or duty;

- references; and

- data about another person.

A partial exemption also exists where the provision of a permanent copy of the information requested would require disproportionate effort.

The topic of employee access to their records is discussed more fully in at 4.18 above.

Dealing with requests to amend an employee's file details

6.15 Under the Act, employees (and others about whom personal data is held) have the right to ask for any inaccuracies in their personal data to be corrected or removed. It is obviously as much in the employer's interests as in the employee's to ensure that the data they hold about staff is accurate and up to date, particularly in light of the fourth data protection principle which expressly requires employers to ensure that the personal data they hold is 'accurate and, where necessary, kept up to date'.

There are three ways in which an employee can seek to have any inaccurate personal data held about them corrected:

- by asking the employer to amend the data;

- by asking the Information Commissioner for an assessment as to whether the processing being carried out by the employer complies with the Act, in which case the Commissioner will decide whether or not to investigate the matter; and

- by applying to a court for an order requiring the employer to correct the inaccuracies or destroy the data.

Although employees have no specific legal right under the Act to demand that their employer rectifies any inaccuracies in the personal data held about them, the requirement on employers to ensure personal data is accurate and kept up to date contained in the fourth data protection principle would create the need to accede to an employee's request to alter any information held that was incorrect.

The most likely instance of an employee wishing for their employer to amend or remove data from their file would be where the file showed that they had been accused of misconduct, for example bullying of a colleague. It would be understandable that the employee would prefer not to have any record of the alleged bullying on their file. The employer may, however, have reasonable grounds to believe that the information recorded on the employee's file is accurate, perhaps on the basis of statements provided by another employee. In these circumstances the employer would not be obliged to remove or delete the file note about the alleged bullying, even in circumstances where the matter had not been proved beyond reasonable doubt. The appropriate action in these circumstances would be for the employer to add a note to the employee's file stating clearly that the employee had refuted the allegations of bullying and did not agree with the employer's version of events or with the statement provided by their colleague.

Employees also have a right to put a request in to their employer asking them to stop, or not to begin, processing personal data about them that is likely to cause substantial damage or distress either to them personally or to another person in circumstances where the damage or distress would be unwarranted. This right is very limited, however, and subject to a range of exceptions, for example where processing is necessary to comply with a legal obligation or required for the performance of a contract. An example of this right in practice could be where an employee did not want their new home telephone number recorded on account of a previous problem with nuisance calls.

To exercise this right, the employee must give their employer written notice asking them to stop the processing that they believe is likely to cause damage or distress, stating a reasonable timescale for the employer to comply with the request. The employer must respond in writing within 21 days, stating either that they will comply with the employee's request or that the request is unjustified and giving the reasons why this view has been taken.

If an employer unreasonably fails to comply with a notice of this kind, the employee can apply to the courts for an order for the employer to stop the processing.

Where an employee has suffered any damage or distress, whether as a result of the recording of information that is inaccurate, the continued processing of information that was likely to cause damage or distress following a request to stop, or as a result of any other breach of the Act, they can seek compensation through the courts.

Records of appraisals, grievances and disciplinary proceedings

6.16 Where performance reviews or appraisals are carried out, whether on a regular or ad hoc basis, the employer will wish to keep records of the review itself and any agreed outcomes such as targets for improvement. Similarly, there will be a need to retain records of any disciplinary action taken against employees and details of any grievances raised.

Performance reviews and appraisals

6.17 Many employers conduct regular performance reviews or annual appraisals in respect of some or all of their employees. Typically this will involve carrying out a review of the employee's job performance over a defined period of time and appraising their future training needs and career development. Appraisal is usually a two-headed process of looking backwards over the past year to analyse past job performance, and looking forwards into the future with a view to improving future job performance. The overall objective of an effective appraisal scheme will be to help each employee to maximise their job performance for the benefit of both the employee and the organisation.

The employee should gain from appraisal a clear understanding of how well they have carried out their job over the past year; a full awareness of where they stand at present; and an insight into what objectives, targets, training, development and career opportunities might be available or planned for the coming year. All of this will require records to be kept. Typically, the record might contain a list of the features of the employee's job with the employee being given a 'rating' against each feature, a summary of training and development needs and agreed plans or new goals and targets for the following year.

As is the case with other types of employment records, the formulation of a record following an appraisal interview should be an open, two-way process between the employee and manager. With openness and transparency being part of the philosophy of the *DPA 1998*, there can be no 'secret reporting' about an employee. The record created following appraisal should not contain any information that is not already known to the employee and should be a fair summary of points that have been discussed at an appraisal interview. If there has been disagreement over a key issue, this fact should also be recorded in order to provide a fair balance.

The right of access under the Act includes access to data that involves the expression of opinions about the employee, for example, the opinion of an employee's line manager that the employee is, or is not, suitable for promotion into a supervisory post.

Grievances

6.18 The handling of grievances raised by employees will similarly involve the processing of personal data about the employee who has raised the grievance, and may possibly include data about another employee, for example if the grievance is about the conduct of a colleague or manager. There will need to be a proper record of the grievance itself (usually written by the employee at the start of the process), a record of any meetings held to try to resolve the grievance, including any appeal meetings, and a record of the outcome.

Disciplinary proceedings

6.19 Whenever any form of disciplinary action is taken against an employee, whether formal or informal, it will be important for the employer to keep a full record.

Informal disciplinary action

6.20 Even if the matter has been handled informally, the employee's manager should, at the very least, record:

- the nature of the problem and the fact that it was brought to the employee's attention;

- the time and date when the manager spoke to the employee; and

- whether there was any outcome, for example the record could simply state that the matter was dealt with informally and there was no outcome, or that an informal oral warning was given.

A copy of the record created by the manager should be given to the employee in order to promote the principle of transparency inherent in the Act. There will be no need for the employee to sign the record, although the employer should record the fact that a copy was given to the employee.

Many managers may not see the need to create a record each time they have words with an employee about unsatisfactory conduct or performance. However, unless a record is kept, the manager will not be in a position to take the matter forward in the event of further misconduct or a failure to improve. Not keeping a record will allow the employee to challenge or deny that they were ever told of the problem at a later stage, and create the risk that any disciplinary action subsequently taken against the employee will not constitute a fair procedure. Furthermore, if the matter escalates and the employee is dismissed, the absence of full records as to how the employer handled the matter will make it very difficult for the employer to succeed in defending a claim of unfair dismissal taken against them at an employment tribunal.

Formal disciplinary action

6.21 If the outcome of the disciplinary proceedings is that the employee receives a formal warning, the warning should state:

- the nature and seriousness of the employee's misconduct;

- the improvement required, or a clear statement that there must be no further instance of misconduct;

- the timescale for improvement;

- the period of time the warning will remain 'live' on the employee's file and what will happen to the warning once it expires (see 6.29 below);

- what will happen if there is no improvement, ie further disciplinary action or dismissal;

- the employee's right to appeal against the warning, how they should appeal and the timescale within which the appeal must be raised.

The warning, together with a record of the disciplinary interview, should be given to the employee and copies of the relevant documents placed in their file.

Security of disciplinary records

6.22 It will, of course, be essential to keep records relating to disciplinary proceedings secure and make sure that they are made available only to those who need access to them as part of their jobs. If the employee has elected to involve a trade union representative or colleague, for example as a companion at a disciplinary interview, the employer should not automatically make the records available to this person but instead should first check with the employee whether that is their wish.

Employees' rights of access to disciplinary records

6.23 Employees have the right of access to all data held about them in connection with disciplinary proceedings. This will include the right of access to:

- any notes made by the employer as part of an investigation into their conduct;

- interview notes or minutes of meetings held in connection with the matter under review;

- copies of any warnings and any other associated documentation placed on the employee's file;

- the expression of any opinion about the employee, for example whether the line manager believes that the employee was, or was not, guilty of a particular offence; and

- information indicating the employer's intentions in respect of the employee.

It is important to recognise that employees have the right of access to such information under the *DPA 1998* even if the disclosure of some of the information might impact on the disciplinary investigation or on prospective disciplinary proceedings. The only exception to the employee's right of access to documents containing information about disciplinary proceedings would be if the information was associated with a criminal investigation and disclosing it to the employee would prejudice that investigation.

The rights of employees under the Act make it essential for the employer to be completely open with the employee throughout any disciplinary investigation and subsequent proceedings. Nothing should be placed on the record that the employee has not already been made fully aware of as a result of face-to-face communication.

Disciplinary investigations

6.24 Unless the facts of an employee's misconduct are undisputed, it will be essential for the employer to carry out a fair and thorough investigation into the alleged misconduct before any decision is made on whether to impose a disciplinary sanction on the employee. Unless and until all the facts relevant to the case are established, the manager dealing with the employee will not be in a position to judge whether the employee's behaviour potentially amounts to misconduct sufficient to justify disciplinary action. Furthermore, if an employee is dismissed without a proper investigation having first been carried out, this will almost certainly have the effect of rendering the dismissal unfair under the *Employment Rights Act 1996, section 98*. The information gathered through the investigation should of course be presented to the employee so that they have the opportunity to make representations before any decision is taken as to whether formal disciplinary action is appropriate. All relevant information obtained as a result of the investigation should be provided to the employee in writing in advance of any disciplinary interview set up to discuss the matter.

It is important to bear in mind that information to be used as evidence to support disciplinary proceedings against an employee must not be gathered by deception. Equally, the person conducting the investigation should not mislead those from whom they seek information in respect of why the information is required and how it will be used.

Whenever an investigation into an incident of alleged misconduct has been carried out, a record will need to be made of the investigation itself and the conclusions drawn from it. It will be important for the record to be accurate, to distinguish between what is known as fact and what is stated as opinion, and to contain sufficient detail to support any conclusions that are drawn from it.

Witness statements

6.25 Where, as part of the investigation, witness statements have been taken from other employees, the employer should seek those employees' consent to the disclosure of the statements to the employee accused of misconduct in order to provide the accused employee with a full and fair opportunity to answer the allegations against them.

If, however, the employee providing the witness statement has a sound reason for not wishing their identity to be disclosed (for example if they have reasonable grounds to fear retaliation from the accused employee), the employer should respect their wishes. Disclosing the witness statement in these circumstances could lead to a breach of confidence and a violation of the data protection rights of the employee who provided the witness statement. In such a case, the employer may, however, be able to disclose the content of the statement without revealing the individual's identity or edit the statement in such a way that the individual's identity is not disclosed. The employer should take a reasoned decision on whether it is reasonable to disclose witness statements in these circumstances, by balancing the witness's right to privacy against the accused employee's right to know the allegations made against them and their source. Further information about disclosing data that would reveal information about third parties is provided at 4.26 above.

The case of *Asda Stores Ltd v Thompson* [2004] IRLR 598 endorses the approach suggested above of blanking out the third party's identity from a document. In this case, the Employment Appeal Tribunal ruled that, for the purpose of disposing of the employees' complaint of unfair dismissal, the

employer had to disclose confidential witness statements involving allegations of drugs dealing, but that they could conceal the identity of the
witnesses, or if necessary edit parts of the statements, in order to prevent
the witnesses from being identified. Employers may wish to bear in mind
that courts and tribunals can (and sometimes do) order the disclosure of
witness statements (and other confidential documents) for the purpose of
disposing fairly with a legal claim.

Accessing information for incompatible purposes

6.26 The second data protection principle states that employers must not
process personal data in any manner that is incompatible with the purpose
or purposes for which the data was originally obtained. When conducting
disciplinary investigations, therefore, the employer must not access or use
information held about employees for the purpose of the investigation if the
original reason for collecting the data was something completely different.
It would, for example, be a breach of the *DPA 1998* to access and read an
employee's emails in order to ascertain whether the employee had made
any remarks relevant to the issue under review unless:

- a policy is in place allowing interception of emails to be carried out for
  this purpose;

- employees have been properly informed about the employer's policy
  of interception; and

- the purpose of the interception is one of those defined as permissible
  in the *Telecommunications* (*Lawful Business Practice*) (*Interception of
  Communications*) *Regulations 2000* (*SI 2000 No 2699*).

If the above conditions are not all met, the employer's only recourse would
be to obtain the employee's express consent before proceeding to read
their emails as part of the disciplinary investigation. Furthermore, reading
an employee's emails without lawful authority to do so would represent a
breach of Article 8 of the *Human Rights Act 1998* (the right to respect for
private and family life, home and correspondence) unless the intrusion into
the employee's privacy could be justified as proportionate in light of the
seriousness of the matter under investigation. An example of circumstances that may justify this course of action could be where an employee
had been accused of sending emails to a colleague that contained sexually
or racially offensive material. In this case it would be proportionate for the
employer to read the employee's emails in order to take the necessary
steps to protect the other employee from unlawful harassment.

Even if the employer has a clear policy in place allowing for the interception
of employees' communications in certain defined circumstances, there is
still a requirement under the Act for data processing to be fair. If, following

a disciplinary investigation, the employee is dismissed, the employer may later have to demonstrate to an employment tribunal that the dismissal was carried out fairly and reasonably. Even though the interception of the employee's emails for the purpose of the investigation might have been *lawful*, this does not necessarily make such interception *fair and reasonable* in relation to the dismissal process. Unless the employee had been informed beforehand (for example as part of the employer's monitoring policy) that their email messages might be intercepted for the purpose of investigating allegations of misconduct, it would be necessary for the employer to obtain their express consent before proceeding to intercept any emails. This is because interception without consent as a means of gathering evidence against the employee would create a serious risk that an employment tribunal could find a subsequent dismissal unfair on procedural grounds on the basis that such a course of action was unreasonable. Once again, openness and transparency form the key to compliance with the relevant legislation.

Records of allegations that are unsubstantiated

6.27 Part 2 of the Employment Practices Code (Employment Records) states that, as a general principle, records of allegations made about employees that have been investigated and found to be without substance should not be retained following the conclusion of the investigation. The Supplementary Guidance points out that there may be exceptions to this general principle, for example if the employee was accused of harassment, bullying or abuse, in which case the employer may wish to keep a limited record of the allegations for their own protection. In this case, the record should show:

- the fact allegations were made and by whom they were made;
- the nature of the allegations;
- the key points that emerged from the investigation;
- what, if anything, was established as fact; and
- the fact that, following an investigation, the allegations were found to be unsubstantiated.

Recording disciplinary interviews

6.28 It can happen that an employee, having been invited to attend a disciplinary interview, brings a tape recorder (or other recording device) along to the meeting with the intention of recording the proceedings. The manager conducting the interview would not be obliged to agree to this and would be entitled simply to advise the employee accordingly. The basic principle applicable in these circumstances is that, for a recording of a workplace discussion to be made, the consent of all parties present would be required.

It would, for the same reason, be impermissible for a manager to make a secret recording of a disciplinary (or grievance) interview conducted with an employee without first obtaining the employee's express consent to the recording being made.

If the employer is willing to agree that a recording should be made of a disciplinary interview, it would be better for the employer to provide and operate the recording equipment, rather than allow the employee to use their own equipment. In this way, the employer would retain control over the data recorded and there would be no possibility of the employee subsequently 'doctoring' the recording. Where a recording is made in this way, the employee should subsequently be given a copy of it.

Spent disciplinary warnings

6.29 The employer should devise and implement a clear procedure on the time periods for which warnings are to remain 'live', and on what is to happen to them when they lapse.

There is no time period laid down in law as to how long disciplinary warnings should remain active on employees' files. It is therefore up to each employer to make their own policy decision on this matter, and to communicate the policy to employees as part of the organisation's overall disciplinary procedure. An employee who receives a warning should also be specifically informed at the time the warning is given how long it will remain 'live' on their file, ie the time period after which the warning will no longer be taken into account for disciplinary purposes. At that point, it must be made clear what will happen to the lapsed warning, for example whether it will:

- be physically removed from the employee's file and destroyed;

- be removed from the employee's file, but a record kept elsewhere of the fact the warning was given, the date it was given, the date it expired and the type of warning (eg first written warning); or

- remain on the employee's file even though it will no longer be taken into account in determining any future disciplinary penalty.

Whilst there would be little point in retaining warnings on file that related to conduct that took place many years earlier, there may be good reason for an employer to want to retain a record of the fact that a warning was given to a particular employee, particularly if the conduct that gave rise to the warning was of a fairly serious nature, or if the same employee had received several warnings over a period of time, indicating a pattern. The employer may legitimately wish to retain some flexibility in their procedures in regard to this matter. Whilst this is acceptable, the employer should always tell the employee, at the time a warning is issued, when it will lapse and what will be done with it at that time.

Another task for the employer in relation to disciplinary warnings is to put in place a reliable system for ensuring that, where their policy provides for the removal or deletion of warnings, this actually takes place on the set dates. A simple diary system may be sufficient for this purpose, given that the number of warnings should not (hopefully!) be too large.

Records of termination of employment

6.30 The employer should keep accurate records of the circumstances leading to employees' termination of employment. A clear distinction should be drawn in the records between a resignation and a dismissal. Furthermore, where an employee is dismissed, the employer should ensure that there is a clear and accurate record of the reason for the dismissal, and that this is consistent with what the employee was told about the reason for their termination. In any event, employees who have one year's service or more have the right under the *Employment Rights Act 1996, section 92* to request a written statement giving particulars of the reason for their dismissal. In the event of such a request, the employer must respond within 14 days. It is sound practice, however, to adopt a policy of providing all employees with a written statement outlining the reason for their dismissal, regardless of length of service and whether or not a request is made.

The reason given should always be the true reason, because if at a later date a claim for unfair dismissal is brought to an employment tribunal, the statement can be used in evidence. At a tribunal hearing for unfair dismissal, the onus is on the employer to show the reason for dismissal, and that it was one of the potentially fair reasons contained in the *Employment Rights Act 1996, section 98.* Thus the written statement giving the reason for the employee's dismissal could support the employer's case, or, if no adequate or potentially fair reason had been provided, considerably weaken the case.

National Staff Dismissal Register

6.31 The Government has recently introduced a National Staff Dismissal Register (NSDR), which lists people who have been dismissed for dishonesty, theft, fraud, forgery or damage to company property. The NSDR, which was approved by the Information Commissioner, applies only to employers in the retail sector.

Records held about individuals on the register, which is accessible online via an encrypted password system, are kept for a five-year period and can include photographs. The records provide information about people who have been dismissed, or have left their jobs whilst under suspicion for acts of dishonesty towards their employer (irrespective of whether or not there has been a prosecution or a conviction). Members of the scheme can search the register to check whether a potential recruit's name is logged there. Only companies that comply with the Information Commissioner's Employment Practices Code are allowed to become members.

Payroll

6.32 The main purpose of any payroll function is to pay employees on time and accurately, so the prime focus of payroll is the employee and thus much personal data about employees will be used for payroll purposes. Employees will expect a high level of confidentiality in respect of their payroll information as the norm. If there are sound procedures in place for the payroll function, these will meet most of the needs of the *DPA 1998*. Nevertheless, it would be advisable from time to time to conduct an assessment of the payroll policies and procedures as measured against the *DPA 1998* and the Employment Practices Code.

Data protection issues in respect of payroll can be classified into two sets:

- the security of the personal data while it is processed in the payroll function; and

- disclosure of the information, whether internally or to external sources.

The first of these two points is a matter for the whole of the organisation. Individual employees themselves generate much payroll-related data. Procedures should be in place to ensure that employees can pass information to the payroll department securely, and that the payroll office and any systems used for payroll data are secure.

Disclosure of payroll-related data outside the payroll function (but still within the organisation) may be required for internal reporting, ranging from the costs of overtime and bonuses to the costs of occupational sick pay. If the information is reported in a way that does not identify individuals, there will be few data protection issues. Where, however, information from which individual employees can be identified is distributed to other parts of the organisation, this must be done within the requirements of the *DPA 1998*. Extra care must be taken where personal data are transferred to parts of the business outside the EEA.

Disclosures outside the organisation are common in the payroll function. Examples include those required by law, such as annual returns to the HM

Revenue and Customs, those required under contract such as returns to pension providers or those instigated by the employees themselves, such as confirmation of earnings for mortgage applications. Employers must ensure that they have the proper authority to justify any disclosure if it is to constitute fair and lawful processing. Adequate security – both technical and organisational – will be needed to prevent unauthorised access or disclosure.

Payroll may also handle sensitive personal data in the course of its work, for example data on employees' trade union membership and medical certificates. This will mean that the employer will have to ensure its payroll department meets the additional data protection conditions applicable to sensitive personal data.

Many employers make use of a third party organisation to manage and handle some elements of the payroll function. Whatever the degree of processing carried out by the third party organisation, the responsibility for data protection remains with the employer. The contract for the processing of payroll must be in writing and must restrict the data processor (the third party organisation) to processing personal data only on the instructions of the data controller (the employer). The data controller must ensure that the data processor has the required level of technical and organisational security. Any obligations imposed on the data controller by law cannot be delegated to the data processor. Thus it is the data controller who must instruct the data processor to make disclosures on behalf of the employer and specify when and how the disclosures are to be made.

In terms of complying with data protection legislation in the areas mentioned above, the key to staying within the law whilst at the same time ensuring fairness, is to:

- adhere to the data protection principles (see CHAPTER 2) and the recommendations contained in the Employment Practices Code; and

- aim to strike a reasonable balance between the needs of the business to operate efficiently and lawfully, and the rights of employees to enjoy privacy and to be treated with respect.

Retention of records

6.33   There is no provision in the *DPA 1998* imposing a time limit on the retention of employment records. However, the fifth data protection principle provides that personal data must 'not be kept for longer than is necessary' taking into account the purpose for which the data was collected in the first place. Thus, it is up to each employer to decide how long to retain employment records, including the files of those whose employment has come to an end. This decision should be based on business needs, taking into account any separate statutory requirements, for example the law relating to the retention of income tax records. Decisions should, of course, be made objectively, and records should not be maintained 'just in case' they might be needed at some future point in time.

Proper policy decisions should therefore be made and adhered to as to the specific retention periods for different types of records, for example the retention of leavers' files (see 6.35 below) or recruitment files (see 5.32 above). Once such policy decisions have been made, they should of course be consistently adhered to and the employer should have in place a system to ensure the regular clearing out of records. This may involve manually 'weeding' out paper-based files on a regular basis (for example once every six months) whilst for computerised records it may be possible to set the computer to flag up information that is due for deletion, or delete it automatically.

Part 2 of the Employment Practices Code states that employers should:

- establish retention times for employment records on the basis of their genuine business needs;

- adopt a risk analysis approach to retention, ie consider whether there would be any realistic risk to the business or to the employees concerned if employment records were deleted or destroyed after a set period of time;

- base any decision to retain employment records on the principle of proportionality;

- treat different records individually or in logical groupings rather than automatically retaining all the information about employees just because there is a need to retain some of it; and

- anonymise information where possible, for example if the employer wishes to hold data for the purpose of reviewing the average length of employment of various groups of staff.

The removal of records should be dealt with carefully and thoroughly so that they are properly destroyed, either by being shredded (in the case of paper records) or permanently deleted from the employer's system and from any servers (in the case of computer records). Furthermore, the employer should not sell on their computers unless they can be confident that all employment records have been fully removed.

Records of foreign nationals' right to work in the UK

6.34 Although the Employment Practices Code recommends that information obtained from a recruitment vetting exercise should be destroyed 'as soon as possible, or in any case within six months', the position with regard to documentary evidence of the successful applicant's right to work in the UK is an exception to this.

Under the *Immigration, Asylum and Nationality Act 2006,* copies of documents obtained for the purpose of proving a job applicant's right to work in the UK must, by law, be retained by the employer throughout employment and then for two years after termination of employment.

Leavers' files

6.35 When employees leave their employment, the employer may legitimately wish to retain their file details for a limited period of time. This will be in case the ex-employee chooses to bring any kind of claim against the employer in an employment tribunal, for example a claim for unfair dismissal. The time limit for most claims to employment tribunals is three calendar months, although in the case of claims for equal pay and for redundancy payments it is six months. The employer would therefore be justified in retaining leavers' records for up to six months. In certain industries, there may be justification for retaining leavers' files for longer periods, for example in the case of employees who worked with hazardous substances.

After this period of time, there may still be sound reasons why the employer may wish to retain a record of the fact that the person was employed, although it will be neither appropriate nor necessary to retain a complete file record of everything that occurred during the person's employment. Different elements of the person's employment record should be treated differently rather than an all-or-nothing approach being adopted. Specific records should be retained only if there is a realistic likelihood that the information may be needed in the future.

An appropriate compromise may be to destroy most of the existing data, but create a new centralised filing system for leavers. Such a system could be set up to record:

- the person's name;

- their address, in case of the need for contact in the future, for example in relation to a reference request;

- some means of ensuring correct identification to guard against the possibility of confusion between two or more leavers with the same name, for example a company reference number or date of birth;

- the dates when the person was employed;

- their job title or designation and department;

- the reasons why their employment ended, for example whether they resigned or were dismissed, and if the latter, the reason for dismissal; and

- space for any comments.

If the employer elects to write any specific comments about the person in the file, they may wish to bear in mind that these comments could be read by the employee at a future date following a subject access request. Nevertheless, this approach should allow employers to retain limited records on leavers without imposing an undue burden on them in relation to their obligations under the Act.

Chapter 7   Health records

Introduction

7.1   Information about workers' health held in the context of employment is an issue that must be treated with care and respect, taking into account the duty of confidentiality owed by employers to their employees in respect of such information. Data about an individual's physical or mental health are regarded as 'sensitive data' under the *Data Protection Act 1998* (*DPA 1998* or 'the Act') and must be treated accordingly. Although the Act does not prevent employers from collecting or using health information about employees, its use must be justified by one of a list of sensitive data conditions. Employers, especially those in the public sector, must also be mindful of the rights contained in Article 8 of the *Human Rights Act 1998*, namely the right to respect for private and family life.

What health records may legitimately be held?

7.2   Information concerning an employee's health may consist of a wide range of data, for example:

- information about current or past illnesses revealed during pre-employment medical screening (see 7.18 below);

- information relating to an individual's disability, including how the particular condition affects the employee (see 7.15 below);

- information on an employee's state of health provided by an employee's GP (with the employee's consent) following a request for a medical report submitted by the employer;

- the results of eye tests carried out in respect of employees who work regularly with display screen equipment;

- an assessment of an employee's fitness for work carried out in order to determine whether they are eligible for permanent health insurance benefit or ill-health early retirement;

- the results of drugs or alcohol testing carried out on employees for safety reasons and held in a personnel file.

When samples are taken, for example as part of drug or alcohol testing, the DPA and the Code of Practice will apply from the point at which the samples yield personal information about the individual.

118

Sensitive data

7.3 As soon as an employer collects information about an employee's physical or mental health or condition, they will be processing 'sensitive data' under the Act. In order for this to be lawful, the employer must be sure that the collection and use of the data satisfies one of the sensitive data conditions set down in the Act.

Conditions for the processing of health information

7.4 The conditions that are potentially relevant to the collection of health records in employment are listed below.

- **Where processing is necessary in order for the employer to comply with a legal obligation in connection with employment.**
  Such a legal obligation may arise as a result of statute or common law, ie decisions of courts and tribunals which interpret the law. There are many legal obligations on employers that may require the processing of sensitive data, for example:

  - health and safety legislation, for example the duty to monitor workers' possible exposure to hazardous materials under the *Control of Substances Hazardous to Health Regulations 2002*;

  - anti-discrimination legislation, including the duty to make reasonable adjustments under the *Disability Discrimination Act 1995*;

  - the duty under the *Social Security Contributions and Benefits Act 1992* to process Statutory Sick Pay for employees who are absent from work due to sickness; to comply with the law, the employer must obtain evidence that the employee is sick and even though the information contained in a 'sick note' may be superficial, it is nevertheless data about the physical or mental health of the employee, and thus sensitive data;

  - unfair dismissal rights contained in the *Employment Rights Act 1996*.

  This list is, of course, not exhaustive.

  The condition would apply whether the legal duty in question related to the individual about whom the sensitive data was held, or to another employee. For example, it may be necessary to record details of a particular employee's physical condition or mental illness in order to protect that person from injury in the workplace, or in order to be able to ensure the safety of others to whom the employer owes a duty of care.

- **Where processing is necessary to protect the vital interests of the employee or another person in circumstances where the employee cannot give consent.**

  This condition is likely to be satisfied only in serious medical emergencies where the health or safety of the employee or another person is at serious risk, thus justifying the disclosure of health information.

- **Where the information has been made public as a result of steps taken by the employee.**

  An example of this could be where an employee has disclosed to a local newspaper that they are suffering from a particular illness in the context (for example) of fund-raising to support research into the illness.

- **Where processing is necessary in connection with any legal proceedings, including the defence of a legal claim against the employer, or necessary for the purpose of obtaining legal advice.**

  This means that if an employee or job applicant has brought a complaint against their employer to court or tribunal, it would be legitimate for the employer to retain details of the employee's health in order to facilitate the employer's defence against the claim. An example could be the retention of an employee's health record in order to defend a claim of disability discrimination brought to tribunal by the employee.

- **Where processing is necessary for medical purposes and is undertaken by a health professional or someone with an equivalent duty of confidentiality.**

  This condition would apply where there is a necessary medical purpose and where health information about employees was held by a company doctor, nurse or similar health professional. It would not be applicable when information on employees' health was held by HR professionals or line managers.

- **Where processing of information about individuals' physical or mental health is for the purpose of carrying out equal opportunities monitoring.**

  If the sole purpose of retaining health data is to promote and maintain equality of treatment, and provided the information is necessary in order to achieve this purpose, it will be lawful to hold the data (see CHAPTER 8 for details of equal opportunities monitoring).

One common thread in most of the above conditions is that it must be *necessary* for the employer to hold the sensitive data in order to fulfil the condition. This means that it is not, for example, open to employers to retain sensitive data about individuals in circumstances where the reason for doing so is convenience or 'just in case' a particular situation might arise.

*Gaining employees' consent to the collection and use of
health information*

7.5 If none of the other conditions for processing sensitive data applies, the only course of action open to an employer who thinks they need to collect and hold information about their employees' health is to obtain individual employees' consent to the processing of sensitive data. However, according to the Information Commissioner's advice, consent to the processing of sensitive data must be 'explicit', and 'freely given'.

Furthermore, the EU Data Protection Directive states of consent:

'... freely given specific and informed indication of his wishes by which the data subject signifies his agreement to personal data relating to him being processed.'

As far as 'freely given' is concerned, it is difficult to imagine there being no adverse consequences to an employee except where the requirement is to sign up to something voluntary. This point is well made in the Employment Practices Code, which, in the context of consent, distinguishes between an existing employee and a job applicant. If, for example, the employer is a transport undertaking and there is a 'no drugs and alcohol' policy enforced by testing, job applicants should be made aware of this as part of their recruitment, ideally early on in the process. This will give the applicant the free choice to accept a job in the knowledge of the drug and alcohol testing that is a condition of that job or to decline because of the condition. An existing employee, on the other hand, may have no realistic choice but to agree to drugs testing if the employer introduced such a policy following consultation.

The issue of consent is explained more fully at 4.7 above.

Who should have access to health records?

7.6 Part 2 of the Employment Practices Code(Employment Records) and the accompanying Supplementary Guidance emphasise that the assessment of health issues, including judgements about an individual's fitness to work, should normally be left to suitably qualified medical personnel, for example an occupational doctor or nurse, or a specialist in a particular condition. In the same way that the income tax and National Insurance implications of a particular expenses payment are best left to the experts in payroll, so too should interpretations of medical information be left to experts. It follows that medical information should only be given to those who can interpret it, and employees' health information should not be widely available. Since line managers and HR professionals are unlikely to be medically qualified, they should not have access to details about an employee's medical condition, nor become involved in the interpretation of medical testing. Instead their access to health information about employees should be restricted to whether or not employees are fit to perform their jobs and whether there are legitimate reasons for employees' absences from work.

For similar reasons, medical information about employees should not be provided to the organisation's payroll department. The occasions when the payroll department will need to know about an employee's ill health will be limited to the payment of statutory and/or contractual sick pay. For this it is only necessary for them to know whether the employee is or is not fit for work under the contract. The payroll department should not, therefore, collect, process or retain any personal data about individual employees' state of health or ill health. Where an employee is leaving the organisation on account of ill-health, for example to take early retirement, payroll department will need to be informed of this fact. Similarly, the payroll department may need to be informed where an employee who is leaving is unable to work the notice period because of ill health. In these circumstances, however, the only information that payroll requires is that the employment is to be terminated due to ill health and the date of termination. The nature of the employee's illness should not be disclosed.

Another recommendation in the Code of Practice is that employees should be informed:

- when information about their health is collected;

- the nature and extent of the health information held about them;

- the reasons for which health information is held; and

- who will have access to the information and in what circumstances.

These points reflect some of the general principles inherent in the *DPA 1998* that data collection and use should be open and transparent.

Where health information is held on employees' personnel files, it will be very important for the employer to ensure a high level of security and confidentiality in respect of these records. It may be advisable to keep information on employees' health separately (see 7.7 below), for example on a separate computer database that is subject to extra-rigorous security controls. Access should then be restricted to those who both have the knowledge to understand the data and the need to know.

The Code of Practice on Workers' Health

7.7 Part 4 of the Employment Practices Code looks at five areas of employee's health:

- general considerations;

- occupational health schemes;

- medical examination and testing;

- drug and alcohol testing; and

- genetic testing.

The Code sets out a number of core principles:

- **It will be intrusive and may be highly intrusive to obtain information about workers' health.**

   This is a simple statement of fact but it acts as a reminder that even for those routinely dealing with personal data and health records, obtaining information about an employee's health will be far from routine for the employee. It follows that any decision on gathering of employees' health data should be taken at the highest level within an organisation. Local managers must not be able to gather health data from employees without consultation with the appropriate central function.

- **Workers have legitimate expectations that they can keep their personal health information private and that employers will respect this privacy.**

   All employees will expect their employer to protect their personal data. In the case of health data, which is much more 'personal' than, for example, an employee's address, employees will expect a greater level of privacy and confidentiality. It should be borne in mind that the eighth Article of the European Convention on Human Rights creates a right of individuals to respect for their private and family life.

   Employees' health records should not be kept physically as part of their personnel files. Ideally a separate filing system should be used so that only health professionals (with their own ethics standards) are able to access the data. There should be a policy on the handling of employees' health records which should identify the different types of health information that may be held within the organisation possibly assigning different levels of confidentiality to the different types. The organisation should:

   – Identify the destination (keeper) of each type of health information so that any data can be quickly and efficiently delivered to their proper destination.

   – Publish the policy throughout the organisation so everyone knows what to do with any medical data they accidentally receive.

   This will also promote amongst employees the organisation's good understanding of employees' concerns about confidentiality of health records.

123

- **If employers wish to collect and hold information on their workers' health, they should be clear about the purpose for which the information will be held and satisfied that this is justified.**

  The third core principle encourages employers to undertake an impact assessment before gathering and using health information about employees.

- **One of the sensitive data conditions must be satisfied** (see 7.4 above).

Impact assessments

7.8 Employers should always consider carefully whether they actually need to collect and hold health information about their employees, and what level of detail is necessary to protect their business interests. If justification for processing health data exists, the employer should still aim to keep the collection and retention of such data to a minimum.

The Employment Practices Code Part 4 (Information about Workers' Health) recommends that employers should conduct an impact assessment to establish whether there is justification for holding information about their employees' health.

Through the impact assessment, the employer can establish what benefits would be gained from processing information about their employees' health, and whether those benefits are sufficient to justify the inevitable adverse impact on employees.

The Code explains that an impact assessment involves:

- identifying the purpose(s) for which health information would be collected and held and the likely benefits (see 7.9 below);

- identifying any likely adverse impact on employees of collecting and holding the information (see 7.10 below);

- considering whether there are less intrusive ways of achieving the employer's objectives (see 7.11 below);

- taking into account the obligations that arise out of the collection and holding of health information; and

- deciding whether or not collecting and holding health information is justified (see 7.12 below).

The purpose of an impact assessment

7.9 The purpose or purposes for which employees' health data are being gathered and used must be assessed in terms of the risks that the purposes address. Many of the risks to the organisation will relate to health and safety issues in respect of its employees, other workers and the general public. The employer will need to consider whether the medical data being collected will address these risks.

Many employers collect information about their workers' health without thinking through why they do so, or what legitimate purpose the information serves. An impact assessment should, as a starting point, identify clearly the purposes for which the employer requires different types and levels of health information about their employees. An 'all-or-nothing' approach will be inappropriate in this context because there will be different risks applicable to different groups of workers. For example, if the employer employs drivers, the need for a high standard of health, fitness and alertness will be greater for the drivers than the fitness threshold required for those doing routine desk-based jobs. The impact assessment should therefore:

- identify the purposes for which health information on different groups of workers will be genuinely necessary;

- specify the type of information that will be necessary to meet the stated purpose(s); and

- clarify that the collection and use of health information will actually be relevant and appropriate to the stated purposes.

Some of the legitimate business purposes for which an employer may wish to hold health data about their employees might be:

- to ensure safety in the workplace;

- to be able to process properly the payment of sick pay, including Statutory Sick Pay;

- to establish employees' entitlement to health-related benefits, for example membership of a health insurance scheme operated by the employer;

- to prevent discrimination against an employee who has a disability;

- to identify when it is necessary to make reasonable adjustments for an employee who has a disability;

- to encourage and maximise attendance and thus reduce costs; and

- to be able to offer support to employees who develop health problems.

The key to compliance with the Act is to be certain that the information collected and retained on employees' files is actually appropriate and relevant to the purpose in question, and not excessive when viewed against the purpose.

Adverse impact

7.10 The collection and use of information about an employee's health will inevitably have an adverse impact on that employee, as it will represent an intrusion into their privacy. It has been accepted in law that the right to respect for privacy (under Article 8 of the *Human Rights Act 1998*) extends into the workplace (see 9.38 below). Employees will therefore have legitimate expectations that their personal health information will remain private. Some employees may also resent the idea of being asked to disclose personal health information, or find the prospect of medical testing during employment embarrassing or demeaning.

The Code of Practice points out that identifying any likely adverse impact means considering:

• the possible consequences of collecting and holding health information on employees' families;

• how extensive the intrusion into the private lives of workers will be as a result of the collection of information about their health;

• the likelihood of those without a business need to know seeing medical data, eg IT staff;

• the possible impact on the relationship of mutual trust and confidence between employee and employer; and

• whether the gathering of the data may be oppressive or demeaning.

In conducting an impact assessment, the employer should therefore seek to identify:

• the likely extent of the adverse impact, ie the consequences for employees of the collection and retention of health information about them;

• the degree of intrusiveness that the employer's health policies and practices will actually create;

• whether information about employees' health is to be disclosed to anyone other than qualified medical practitioners, eg to HR staff or IT workers involved in maintaining employees' files, thus causing potential discomfort amongst employees;

• whether the trust and confidence in the employment relationship could be threatened by the collection of health information; and

• whether the collection of health information could be embarrassing or demeaning for employees.

Minimising the intrusion into employees' privacy

7.11   Assuming that the employer has established that there is a genuine business need to collect certain information about their employees' health, they should then seek to establish what steps can be taken to ensure the minimum degree of intrusiveness. The employer should take steps to minimise the intrusion into employees' privacy by:

- taking all reasonable steps to minimise exposure to hazardous substances in the workplace, in order to remove or reduce the need for medical testing;

- ensuring that their practices of collecting and using health information about employees are not any more intrusive than is absolutely necessary to meet the employer's stated business objectives, for example using medical questionnaires would be less intrusive than conducting a physical health check;

- targeting medical testing, for example drugs screening, only at employees who work in safety-critical jobs or following an incident or accident, rather than testing everyone;

- restricting the numbers of staff who have access to health information about employees to medically qualified staff only;

- designing medical testing to reveal the minimum amount of health information that is required for the purpose for which the testing was undertaken; and

- devising systems and procedures that allow employees to communicate confidentially with any occupational health professionals, ie so that staff know that certain types of communications will not be monitored.

Justification for processing health information

7.12   The key purposes of carrying out an impact assessment will be so that the employer can decide whether there is justification for them to collect information about their employees' health, and if so how much information needs to be collected and the purposes for which it will be used. It should not be assumed that there is a business need for collecting and/or retaining detailed health records on all staff, but instead the employer should adopt an open-minded approach and examine:

- what the purposes of collecting and holding health information would be;

- whether the type of information the employer proposes to collect and hold would actually achieve those purposes;

- whether the collection and use of health information would produce benefits for the business that outweighed the adverse impact to employees;

- whether there are any alternatives to the methods proposed to collect health information that would be less intrusive to employees (see 7.11 above); and

- whether there has been a full process of consultation with trade unions, with employee representatives or with employees directly prior to the introduction of any new policy on medical screening.

Impact assessments need not be formal and lengthy processes and may be a simple mental assessment. However, whenever the balance is in favour of processing health records, it is strongly advisable to write down the assessment. Clearly this will be particularly important in the more intrusive cases.

Sickness and absence records

7.13 The Employment Practices Code, Part 2 (Employment Records) recommends that employers should keep sickness records separately from absence records. Sickness records will provide information about employees' health, for example the reason why a particular employee was absent from work at a particular time, or information about a particular employee's illness and its effects on him or her. Such records will, as stated above, be classed as sensitive data under the *DPA 1998*. Absence records (or attendance records), on the other hand, will show only the dates of employees' absences and the fact they were attributable to sickness (or injury) without giving any information on the specific medical condition or injury that caused them.

The Code of Practice also suggests that the employer should use absence records (rather than sickness records) whenever possible. For example if a line manager wished to review information about the overall patterns of absence or lengths of absences of a group of employees, the absence record should be sufficient. In contrast, if the line manager needed to review an individual's record in order to investigate frequent or persistent short-term absences, or a single long-term absence, it may be justifiable for the manager to be granted access to the individual's sickness record. Managing attendance is a key line management responsibility and line managers will need certain information at certain times if they are to ensure the efficient running of their departments. If information about an employee's health or sickness is necessary for the manager to carry out their managerial role, then its disclosure for that purpose will be potentially justifiable, depending of course on the circumstances of the individual case.

Information contained in sickness records should generally not be disclosed to non-medical personnel unless one of the sensitive data conditions is satisfied (see 7.4 above).

The fourth data protection principle in the *DPA 1998* requires that data are held only as long as is necessary. This principle is no different in the case of health records. Where an organisation has carried out medical examinations or testing, they should retain for audit purposes only records about the administration of the medical examinations or testing (dates, numbers involved, etc) and not the medical information obtained.

The Access to Medical Reports Act 1988

7.14 Sometimes an employer may wish to seek information from an employee's GP or consultant about a particular health issue affecting the employee's ability to perform their job. In this case the *Access to Medical Reports Act 1988* will apply.

Under the *Access to Medical Reports Act 1988,* employers are not allowed to apply to an employee's GP for a medical report unless they have first obtained the employee's written consent. Employees have the statutory right to refuse such consent under the Act and the employer must respect this right.

The employer should proceed as follows if the organisation wishes to obtain a medical report about an employee from the employee's GP or specialist:

- notify the employee in writing that the employer wishes to apply to the employee's doctor for a medical report;

- inform the employee of their right to withhold consent for the application to be made;

- inform the employee of their other rights under the *Access to Medical Reports Act 1988*;

- obtain the employee's written consent for the application to be made; and

- inform the doctor to whom any request for a medical report is sent if the employee has stated an intention to seek access to the report before it is forwarded to the employer.

If an employer has a valid reason for requesting an employee's consent to apply to their GP for a medical report, the employer should seek only that information which is relevant and necessary from the GP. Employees should not be asked to consent to the disclosure of their entire health record, as this would be excessive and unnecessarily intrusive. Instead the employer should devise specific and relevant questions to pose to the GP and ensure that the information requested is relevant to the employee's ability to perform the job for which they are employed. When writing to the doctor to request a medical report, the employer should remember to enclose a copy of the employee's consent form or letter.

A summary of employees' rights under the *Access to Medical Reports Act 1988* are:

- to refuse to give consent for the employer to contact their GP for a report;

- to gain access to any medical report prepared about them by their GP or consultant and to be given or allowed to take a copy of the report;

- to ask the doctor to amend the report, if it is inaccurate or misleading in any way; and

- to refuse to allow the report, once prepared, to be passed to the employer.

The *Access to Medical Reports Act 1988* does not normally apply to medical reports prepared by occupational doctors. This is because this Act's provisions cover only reports 'relating to the physical or mental health of the individual prepared by a medical practitioner who is or has been responsible for the clinical care of the individual'. For this reason, it is often more convenient for employers to use occupational doctors to provide advice on employees' general health and fitness to work.

Employees and job applicants who have a disability

7.15 The *Disability Discrimination Act 1995* (*DDA 1995*), which applies to all employers irrespective of size, defines a disabled person as someone who 'has a physical or mental impairment which has a substantial and long-term adverse effect on his ability to carry out normal day-to-day activities'. 'Long-term' in this context means 12 months or more. The *DDA 1995* thus covers:

- a range of physical illnesses, conditions and injuries;

- any mental illness or condition including many stress-related illnesses;

- progressive conditions such as muscular dystrophy or Alzheimer's disease from the point at which the illness is having some adverse effect on the individual;

- multiple sclerosis, cancer and HIV, which are automatically regarded as disabilities from the point of diagnosis irrespective of the level of effect on the individual;

- recurring conditions, even during periods of remission, provided the condition is likely to recur;

- conditions that fluctuate between minor and substantial; and

- past disabilities.

It is important to recognise that someone who is disabled does not necessarily have poor health, as the disability may have occurred as a result of an injury, or may be the result of a condition the individual was born with, for example a hearing impairment. Nevertheless, as can be seen from the above list, physical and mental illnesses may constitute disabilities for the purposes of the *DDA 1995*, depending on how long the particular illness has lasted (or is likely to last) and whether its effect on the individual's day-to-day life is 'substantial'.

Apart from the duty in the *DDA 1995* not to treat an employee or job applicant unfavourably on grounds related to a disability, there is also an important duty on employers to make reasonable adjustments to their working arrangements, working practices and premises in order to accommodate the needs of the particular disabled person. A failure to meet this duty will render employers liable to claims of disability discrimination.

If an employer is to be in a position to fulfil its obligation under the *DDA 1995* to make reasonable adjustments for an employee or job applicant with a disability, it will be necessary for them to collect and retain data about the individual's condition and its effects on their ability to perform their job. The collection of such data will be justified under the provision in the *DPA 1998* that allows employers to process sensitive data if it is necessary to do so in order to comply with a legal obligation (see 7.4 above).

Clearly, the disabled person will have a more in-depth knowledge of their condition, its effects and what measures would be likely to help them at work than any HR practitioner or line manager. It follows that the employer should initiate open discussions with the disabled employee (or job applicant) as to what adjustments would help them, and adopt a supportive approach.

Some examples of adjustments that employers may wish to consider in relation to an employee who has had frequent or extensive sickness absences on account of a condition that amounts to a disability could be to:

- allow the disabled employee to take more time off work than would normally be acceptable, for example to attend regular medical appointments;

- look into the possibility of alternative employment that the employee could do;

- alter the employee's job duties, or allocate some of the duties to another employee if, as a result of a disability, the employee cannot carry out those duties or has difficulty carrying them out;

- adjust working hours, for example by providing additional or longer rest breaks if the employee's illness causes them to tire easily;

- allow an employee who is beginning to recover from an illness to work part-time or work partly from home for a temporary period in order to ease them back into full-time employment.

Further examples of reasonable adjustments that employers should consider are to be found in 8.15 below.

Medical screening

7.16 In order to promote safe and healthy working, an employer may wish to conduct medical screening on their existing employees and also on job applicants to whom it is intended to make an offer of employment. As with any fair and lawful data gathering, employees will need to know about how their health information will be used and who will have access to it both inside and outside the organisation. Generally, when individuals give information to a health professional, they expect that the information will remain confidential and not be passed to others.

Medical examinations during employment

7.17 It is common for employers to exercise the right (through clauses written into employees' contracts of employment) to require their employees to undergo a medical examination with a company-nominated doctor either on a regular basis (for example every three years) or at the employer's request. Although the *DPA 1998* does not cover the issue of whether medical examinations or medical testing is legitimate or desirable, the Act does come into play whenever the results of a medical examination are recorded, including the retention of samples that can be tracked back to an individual employee. Similarly, the Employment Practices Code does not address how those examining and testing employees should conduct themselves. Medical examinations and testing should, however, be carried out by suitably qualified health professionals who will be bound by their own professional codes of conduct especially in their responsibility to the employee for a duty of confidentiality.

Employees' consent to undergo medical examinations with a company-nominated doctor should therefore cover not only the medical screening itself, but also the production of a medical report and the subsequent recording of the information. This approach can be advantageous for employers since a company doctor will have more thorough knowledge than the employee's GP of the employer's business requirements and whether or not the particular employee's job involves any specific physical or psychological demands that might require the employee to have a higher than normal level of health or fitness. The issue of employee consent is explained further at 4.7 above.

Where it is the employer's policy to require employees to undergo medical screening with an occupational doctor, they should:

- ensure the employer's policy on medical screening and any associated rules and standards are clearly communicated to all staff;

- set out the circumstances in which medical examinations or testing may be required, for example whether the rules apply to all staff, or only to staff in certain jobs, and whether testing is conducted on a routine basis or whenever the employer deems it appropriate;

- ensure the policy states the nature of the testing, for example whether it is a general health check or whether it is also designed to detect specific conditions or exposure to defined substances or drugs use (see 7.20 below);

- explain fully the consequences for employees of refusing to agree to be tested, and the consequences if a test proves positive or negative;

- inform employees how information obtained through testing will be used and to whom it may be disclosed;

- be sure that samples of blood, urine, etc, provided by employees are not tested for any condition or substance unless the employee concerned has given their free and explicit consent to the particular type of test;

- refrain from using or recording any information that comes to light by chance during medical testing, for example if a routine medical examination revealed that an employee was pregnant, this fact should not be recorded or used by the employer in any way; and

- destroy all medical data as soon as there is no further need to keep it.

The employee will be entitled to a copy of any reported findings from an examination or test. It is therefore advisable whenever samples are taken that pairs are taken in order to provide a sample for the employee.

The Employment Practices Code suggests that employers should conduct medical examinations on existing employees only on a voluntary basis, or where they are satisfied that testing is a necessary and justified measure to:

- prevent a significant risk to health and safety;

- determine employees' fitness for carrying out their jobs;

- determine whether an employee is fit to return to work after a period of sickness absence;

- establish employees' entitlement to health-related benefits, for example payment of sick pay; and

- prevent discrimination against an employee who has a disability, or assess what reasonable adjustments might be made to support the employee.

Pre-employment medical screening

7.18 Many employers require all new recruits to undergo a pre-employment medical examination prior to confirming their appointment. This is generally legitimate in order to ensure that the person is sufficiently fit and healthy to perform the job in question and possibly to determine whether they will be eligible to join any pension or health insurance scheme operated by the employer. The Employment Practices Code suggests, however, that employers should:

- carry out medical screening only on the person whom they intend to appoint (and not on other shortlisted candidates);

- identify and record the specific business purpose(s) for which the medical examination is being carried out;

- consider whether there is a less intrusive way of meeting their business objectives, the most obvious example being to use a medical questionnaire (see 7.19 below) rather than requiring the candidate to undergo a medical examination; and

- inform all job applicants at an early stage during the recruitment process that the successful applicant will be required to undergo a medical examination or complete a medical questionnaire and that any offer of employment will be conditional on the results of these being satisfactory to the employer.

The employer should also seek to ensure that medical examinations cover only those aspects of employees' health and fitness that are relevant to their ability to perform the jobs into which they are being appointed.

Using medical questionnaires

7.19 Asking employees or job applicants to complete a medical questionnaire will be considerably less intrusive than requiring them to undergo a medical examination. This approach should therefore be used whenever possible as an alternative to a medical examination, or as a first stage in order to establish whether a full medical examination is necessary.

Employers who use medical questionnaires should review them in order to make sure that they ask only for information that the employer needs for a stated legitimate purpose. Information that is not relevant and necessary should not be requested. It may be appropriate to have two or more versions of the questionnaire to be used in respect of different jobs.

The best way forward for an employer that wishes to use medical question-naires to collect health information about their employees or job applicants would be to have the questionnaire designed (or at the very least reviewed and edited) by an occupational doctor. The information provided by employees or job applicants on the questionnaire should also be inter-preted only by qualified medical practitioners, and not (for example) by an HR officer.

Drugs and alcohol testing

7.20 Before contemplating introducing a policy of drugs and/or alcohol testing, the employer should be quite certain that there are legitimate grounds for implementing such a policy. The retention of results, including samples, following a drugs or alcohol test will fall squarely under the *DPA 1998* and will of course also have considerable implications under Article 8 of the *Human Rights Act 1998* (the right to respect for private life).

One underlying principle is that the purpose of any drugs and/or alcohol screening programme in employment should be about assessing the competence of an employee to perform a specific job, and not a way of controlling off-duty behaviour, if the employee's work is unlikely to be affected. Employers should therefore (wherever possible) seek to use tests that are designed to identify impairment at work rather than more general tests that identify the use of (illegal) substances in an employee's private life.

For employers who already have a drugs/alcohol screening programme in place, it may be advisable to review it in order to ascertain whether its application in its present form is justified. If the employer conducts drugs/alcohol testing without having a proper business reason to do so, it is likely that any resultant dismissal on account of a positive test result would be found unfair by an employment tribunal.

Drugs or alcohol testing and the retention of results will be particularly intrusive for employees. The purpose for carrying out the testing must therefore be proportionate in light of the employer's real business needs. Urine analysis, for example, will reveal not only the presence of certain illegal drugs in the employee's body, but may also bring to light the existence of other medical conditions.

Normally, the only grounds that will justify drugs/alcohol testing at work will be for the purpose of ensuring safety. Thus routine testing should be limited to employees whose jobs are safety-critical, for example those who work with heavy machinery, employees whose jobs involve intense concentration or those who have responsibility for the care of others (for example drivers). Otherwise, the only justification for testing an employee whose job did not fall into the safety-critical category would be if there were reasonable grounds to suspect that the employee was under the influence of drugs or alcohol whilst at work, and that this state of affairs was likely to have a negative impact on safety or performance. Even then, the employer would be obliged to consider whether a less intrusive test could be used to determine whether the employee was impaired, for example by using a test that measured speed of reaction.

A measured approach to policy formulation should always be taken, bearing in mind the need for proportionality. This means that the employer should think carefully whether the testing and methods proposed are appropriate, relevant and necessary in relation to the purpose for which testing is proposed.

It is important to bear in mind that under the *DPA 1998*, random drugs or alcohol screening of all employees in the business will not be justified on the grounds that some of the employees perform safety-critical roles. It will not be valid to argue that everyone (for example administrative staff who perform desk-based jobs) should be subjected to random testing in order to promote fairness and consistency. This argument cannot be sustained because it does not make sense to treat everyone in the same way when the circumstances of employees' jobs are completely different. Blanket policies on testing should therefore be avoided.

Equally, it will not normally be justifiable to conduct drugs or alcohol screening on an employee for performance-related or conduct reasons, unless there is also a safety issue at stake.

If an employer has established (ideally through an impact assessment – see 7.8 above) that drugs and/or alcohol screening is necessary and appropriate in order to ensure health and safety, there will be certain important steps that they will have to take to ensure their practices remain within the law:

- consult employees or their representatives before deciding to introduce a drugs or alcohol screening programme;

- consult qualified experts before finalising the type of testing to be used;

- institute clear guidelines informing employees of the purpose of the drugs or alcohol screening programme and what the tests are designed to detect;

- ensure drugs testing is carried out and interpreted only by qualified and competent professionals who can provide guarantees that they will meet appropriate standards of quality, integrity, confidentiality and security;

- adopt a policy of testing only for substances that are likely to impact on health and safety at work and a level of exposure that is likely to cause impairment;

- seek, where possible, to use tests that detect only recent exposure to the substances being tested for;

- aim to use the least intrusive method possible to achieve the stated business purpose;

- minimise the amount of personal data that is collected during drugs or alcohol testing; and

- review whether it is possible to use tests of cognitive ability instead of drugs or alcohol testing, for example a test that measures hand–eye coordination and response times.

It will be important also for the employer to communicate clearly to all employees who are subjected to drugs or alcohol testing what will happen if they fail a test. Other company procedures will have to be amended, where appropriate, to make reference to this, for example the employer's disciplinary procedure will have to make it clear if an employee who tests positive will be subjected to disciplinary action or dismissed (see 7.22 below).

Finally, of course, the consent of employees will be required before any drugs screening can be lawfully carried out. This can be obtained by incorporating both the drugs/alcohol screening policy and the requirement to undergo screening into employees' contracts of employment. Otherwise any drugs or alcohol screening programme would have to be conducted on a purely voluntary basis. Consent should, of course, include the employee's permission for the employer to process any data that are obtained as a result of the drugs or alcohol test.

Selecting employees for testing

7.21 Where drugs or alcohol screening is conducted on a random basis, it will be important to ensure that the methods used to select employees for screening are truly random, and include everyone within the group of staff for whom testing is considered necessary (for example managers should not be excluded solely on the basis that they are considered too 'senior'). If testing is to be conducted on a 'with cause' basis only, employees should be clearly informed of the criteria that will be used to trigger a test, usually an incident or accident or possibly where the employee's behaviour is observed to be unusual or erratic or where performance has notably declined without any obvious explanation.

Dismissal following a positive test result

7.22 Where an employer has a drugs and/or alcohol screening programme in place, the employer will have to decide what action to take in the event that an employee fails a test. Two different approaches are possible:

- implementing a programme of rehabilitation and support for the employee if the employee agrees; or

- disciplinary action up to and including dismissal.

Dismissal for testing positive may be fair provided that all of the following conditions are met:

- there is a contractual right to carry out drugs or alcohol screening;

- there were reasonable grounds for requiring the employee to submit to a test, ie either as a result of a screening programme implemented for safety-related reasons or because the employee has shown signs of impairment whilst at work;

- health or safety may be put at risk or there is likely to be substantial damage to the employer's reputation; and

- the employer's rules provide for dismissal on account of a positive test result, including where the drugs have been taken outside of working time.

Dismissal may also be fair where the employer has a contractual right and a proper reason to require employees to undergo drugs or alcohol screening and the employee has refused to submit to a test without good reason.

The fairness of any dismissal will depend on all the circumstances of the individual case and in particular whether the employer has handled the matter in a reasonable way. One case that dealt with dismissal on account of a positive test result was *O'Flynn v Airlinks the Airport Coach Co Ltd* [2002] EAT 0269/01. In this case, the employee worked as a customer care assistant, but her job occasionally involved assisting drivers to manoeuvre coaches and serving hot drinks on moving coaches. The employer had introduced an alcohol and drugs policy and random screening, details of which had been well communicated to all staff. The policy ruled that employees were prohibited from having drugs or alcohol in their systems whilst at work, and that a positive drugs test would lead to disciplinary action and possibly dismissal. Some five months after the introduction of the policy, the employee was selected for a random drugs test, and admitted to having taken drugs in her own time. The test proved positive for cannabis. The employee was consequently dismissed following a disciplinary interview. She claimed unfair dismissal.

The EAT upheld the employment tribunal's decision that the dismissal was fair. Although the case occurred prior to the implementation of the *Human Rights Act 1998*, the EAT elected to consider the effect Article 8 of the European Convention on Human Rights (the right to respect for private life) might have had on the decision. They found that the drugs screening policy infringed the employee's right to a private life to the extent that it meant that certain drugs could not be taken in her own time without jeopardising her employment, and because it required her to provide a urine sample if she was randomly selected for screening. Nevertheless, the EAT held that the policy and the testing were necessary and appropriate for reasons of public safety, and that the employee's dismissal following the positive test result and her admission that she had taken drugs was not disproportionate in light of the safety issues at stake.

Genetic testing

7.23 Genetic testing should generally not be used by employers. Genetic testing is still under development and cannot normally predict reliably if an individual will in fact develop a particular disease or condition during their working life, nor (if the person does develop the condition), how severely it will affect the individual. Because of this, it would be inappropriate to base employment decisions on such testing. Genetic testing would, in any event, be extremely intrusive and would normally not therefore be justifiable in the employment context.

The only exception to this general principle would be in a situation where factors in the workplace were known to pose particular risks to those with particular genetic variations. In this case, genetic testing might be justified in order to alert the employer (and any employee who is vulnerable) to the possibility that an individual might be at risk. This would only be valid, however, if the type of test used was likely to be reliable in detecting the genetic condition in question, and even if this was the case, the link between a particular hazard in the workplace and the individual's susceptibility to it would be unlikely to represent a certainty.

The Employment Practices Code suggests that:

- genetic testing should be used only as a last resort if there is no other way of minimising particular risks to health inherent in the workplace;

- genetic testing should not be used to try to predict an employee's future general health;

- employers should not require individuals to take a genetic test as a condition of employment (as advised also by the Human Genetics Commission);

- genetic testing should be used only if it is clear that an employee with a particular, detectable genetic condition would be likely to pose a serious safety risk to others or if the specific working environment or practice might pose specific risks to employees with particular genetic variations;

- genetic testing should be contemplated only if there is scientific evidence that the particular test is valid for the purpose for which it is to be used; and

- employees should not be required to disclose the results of previous genetic testing they have undertaken, eg to a potential new employer.

Where, despite the above concerns, an employer believes that there is solid justification for carrying out genetic testing of employees and/or job applicants, the results of the specific genetic tests should be communicated directly to the employee concerned. The employer should also ensure in these circumstances that the employee has access to professional medical advice.

Chapter 8   Equality and equal opportunities monitoring

Introduction

8.1   Any employer who wants their business to succeed will place the promotion of equal opportunities high up on their management agenda priority listing. Taking steps to promote equality of opportunity amongst all staff and to ensure the workplace is free from all forms of discrimination will help the organisation to retain and motivate their staff and create a working environment in which employees feel comfortable. Employees who feel comfortable, ie reassured that they will be treated with respect and not become the victims of any unfavourable treatment, including harassment, will be enabled to perform to the best of their abilities. The promotion of equal opportunities in the workplace will be particularly important so as to ensure that people from minority groups are treated fairly and equally in every respect, both during the process of recruitment and once employed.

An employer who devises and implements clear policies on equal opportunities and the prohibition of all forms of discrimination and harassment will thus go a long way to combating unfairness, prejudice and bullying and help to create an environment of mutual trust and respect in which workers can exercise their talents fully to the benefit of the employer.

Equal opportunities monitoring

8.2   In order to ensure equal opportunities in the workplace, many employers conduct monitoring. Monitoring may be done in relation to the numbers and composition (in terms of gender, racial or ethnic origin, age, disability and possibly religion and sexual orientation) of:

- successful and unsuccessful job applicants;

- staff who receive training;

- employees who have been promoted;

- employees who benefit or suffer detriment as a result of performance assessment;

- staff who are the subject of disciplinary action;

- staff who raise grievances; and

- employees who leave the organisation (possibly divided into those who resign and those who are dismissed).

The key purposes of monitoring will be to:

- analyse the reasons for any differences in treatment of different 'groups' of staff and ensure these reasons are not linked directly or indirectly to gender, race or age;

- audit the processes of recruitment to ensure that the composition of the numbers of staff being shortlisted and selected (for example in terms of racial group) is proportionate to that of the total number of people applying for posts;

- check that there is no disparate impact on different groups of staff as a result of the organisation's policies and procedures, for example the ways in which grievance and disciplinary procedures are applied;

- discover whether there any barriers to equality of opportunity in appraisal, training and promotion;

- identify areas where change is needed; and

- take action to deal with any inequalities discovered as a result of monitoring.

The investigation and record keeping associated with monitoring is naturally controversial as it requires employers to seek to obtain personal information about individuals and to distinguish between individuals based on this information. Some people may object to being asked questions about, for example, their religion or belief, on the basis that the question represents an intrusion into their private lives. It should be borne in mind, however, that it is the motive for which information is sought and kept and the purpose to which the information is put that are important. Nowadays there is a wide acceptance that the information and record keeping required for equal opportunities monitoring represents a valid and useful tool for identifying and tackling discrimination and promoting equal opportunities.

In the public sector, monitoring in respect of the racial origin of job applicants and employees is compulsory (see 8.13 below).

Responsibility for equal opportunities monitoring

8.3 As part of the process of equal opportunities monitoring, the employer should nominate a senior person within the organisation to be responsible for planning, designing and carrying out monitoring, and for ensuring that the record keeping associated with monitoring complies with the *Data Protection Act 1998* (*DPA 1998* or 'the Act').

The person appointed to hold such responsibility should, ideally, be some-one who has the authority to challenge and change any procedures or practices that are found to have a discriminatory impact.

Equal opportunities monitoring and the DPA 1998

8.4 Information gathered about individuals' gender, racial or ethnic origin, religion or belief, age, sexual orientation (if monitored) and disability will constitute personal data under the *DPA 1998*. Information obtained as a result of equal opportunities monitoring must therefore be treated in accordance with the provisions of the Act and the Employment Practices Data Protection Code.

Some of this information will constitute 'sensitive data' and thus require special treatment (see 8.5 below). The employer is required to abide by all the data protection principles when processing such data and will also, for example, have to:

- inform staff how and why their data will be used;

- inform staff to whom the data will be disclosed; and

- ensure the security of the data.

When data gathered for monitoring purposes constitutes sensitive data

8.5 Some of the information that will be required to conduct monitoring is regarded under the *DPA 1998* as sensitive data, in particular, information about individuals':

- racial or ethic origin;

- religious beliefs or other beliefs of a similar nature;

- physical or mental health or condition;

- sexual orientation; and

- trade union membership.

When it is lawful to process sensitive data in relation to monitoring

8.6 As a general principle, the *DPA 1998* states that employers may not process sensitive data about an individual unless either the person has consented to processing, or one of a limited number of conditions is fulfilled.

DPA 1998, Schedule 3 contains a list of the conditions that may justify the processing of sensitive data, but in relation to the types of sensitive data listed above, the only conditions likely to be relevant would be:

- where processing is necessary in order for the employer to comply with a legal obligation in connection with employment;

- where processing is necessary in connection with any legal proceedings, including the defence of a legal claim against the employer; and

- where processing of information about individuals' racial or ethnic origin is for the purpose of carrying out equal opportunities monitoring with a view to promoting and maintaining equality of treatment, and the information is necessary in order to achieve this purpose. The Act adds another condition relevant to this provision which is that the processing must be carried out with appropriate safeguards in place to ensure the rights and freedoms of the individuals.

The processing of information about gender or age does not constitute sensitive data under the Act and employers are therefore free to conduct monitoring on these features without any particular restraints or conditions.

Obtaining consent

8.7   If employers wish to monitor their staff in respect of features other than racial/ethnic origins, and if the information they wish to collect is not necessary to comply with a legal obligation in connection with employment or for conducting any legal proceedings, they will essentially have to obtain the consent of their employees to the processing.

Under data protection principles, consent to the processing of sensitive data must be 'explicit', and 'freely given'. 'Explicit' in this context means that the employee must have signed a document indicating their agreement, having first been clearly informed how the information will be used. 'Freely given' is described as giving the employee a genuine choice as to whether or not to consent to the processing, and operating a policy of not subjecting anyone who declines to give their consent to any detriment. Part 2 of the Employment Practices Code (Employment Records) points out that the extent to which individuals' consent can be relied on in the context of employment is limited on account of this requirement for consent to be freely given.

Despite the fact that it may not always be a sound prospect for an employer to rely on consent as a means of justification for the processing of sensitive data about their employees, it is nevertheless a sensible precaution for an employer as a matter of course to seek employees' (and job applicants') consent to the collection and use of sensitive data about them.

Consent from job applicants for the employer to process information about them, including sensitive data, can be obtained during the process of recruitment either by including an appropriate statement on the application form for the applicant to sign, or by using a specially designed form which the applicant is asked to sign, for example at the time of a recruitment interview (see 5.23 above for further information about obtaining consent from job applicants).

Obtaining consent from existing employees, for example where an employer decides to commence equal opportunities monitoring for the first time, could be obtained by placing an appropriately worded clause on the equal opportunities monitoring form for each employee to sign when they complete the form. The form should also explain clearly the purpose for which the data will be used.

The employer should, in any event, always assess whether there is justification for seeking any sensitive data from employees or job applicants, and explain properly why the information is being requested and how it will be used. It should also be a part of the monitoring policy that any employee who declines to provide the information requested by the employer is not penalised in any way (unless the information is needed for legal reasons – see 8.8 and 8.9 below).

An alternative way forward, which would avoid the need for consent altogether, would be to conduct monitoring of existing employees in an anonymised way, ie by asking employees to complete an equal opportunities monitoring form without disclosing their identity. This approach may not, however, be altogether satisfactory as there would be no method of checking whether the individuals who chose to supply the information had supplied it fully and accurately. There might also be a substantial proportion of the workforce who would choose not to return the form at all.

Where the processing of sensitive data is necessary in order to comply with a legal obligation

8.8   One of the conditions that justifies the processing of sensitive data is if the data is necessary in order for the employer to comply with a legal obligation in connection with employment. Such a legal obligation may arise as a result of statute or common law, ie decisions of courts and tribunals which interpret the law. The scope of this condition is fairly wide in the context of employment. For example, it would be relevant to public sector organisations who are obliged by law to conduct monitoring in respect of their employees' racial and ethnic origins (see 8.13 below).It is important to note, however, that, in order to fulfil this condition, processing must be *necessary* to comply with a legal obligation and not merely convenient or desirable from the employer's point of view.

Equality and equal opportunities monitoring

The following is a list of possible legal obligations that could potentially justify the processing of sensitive data that might be used also for monitoring purposes:

- Information about a worker's health or disability may be necessary to comply with the provisions of the *Disability Discrimination Act 1995* (see 8.14 below), in particular the duty to make reasonable adjustments. The employer may wish also to monitor equality of opportunity by checking (for example) whether staff with disabilities are promoted or transferred at the same rate as non-disabled people.

- Information about health or disability will also be necessary to allow the employer to process Statutory Sick Pay. The employer may also wish to conduct monitoring in relation to the sickness records of various groups of staff, for example men and women, people from different racial groups, etc in order to ensure equality of treatment.

- Information about employees' health may be necessary for the employer to fulfil their duties under the *Health and Safety at Work Act 1974*, ie so that the employer can take the appropriate and necessary steps to ensure the health, safety and welfare of all their employees at work.

- Information about trade union membership will be necessary to enable the employer to deduct members' subscriptions from their pay at source.

- Information about an employee's previous criminal convictions may be necessary in relation to certain sensitive posts in order to ensure the safety of, for example, children or vulnerable adults (see 5.16 above for further information). Certain public sector bodies may also have specific statutory duties imposed on them in relation to the qualifications or background of their employees.

- Information about individuals' racial and ethnic origins, religion or belief, sexual orientation and disability, all of which are governed by anti-discrimination legislation, may be processed because of the duty placed on every employer not to discriminate on any of the prohibited grounds against job applicants or employees.

- Information about employees' racial and ethnic origin is required for public authority employers to fulfil their duties under the *Race Relations Act 1976*. The *Race Relations Act 1976 (Statutory Duties) Order 2001* imposed a duty on public sector employers to carry out regular monitoring of the racial balance of their employees and all applicants for employment, training and promotion (see 8.13 below for further information).

- Information about job applicants' nationality may be necessary at the time of recruitment in order for the employer to avoid being in breach of the *Immigration, Asylum and Nationality Act 2006* (by employing someone who does not have the right to work in the UK). Although nationality is not, in itself, regarded as sensitive data, it is often inextricably linked with individuals' racial origins. This subject is explored more fully at 5.29 above).

Where the processing of sensitive data is necessary in connection with legal proceedings

8.9 The *DPA 1998* states that an employer may process sensitive data if such processing is necessary in connection with any legal proceedings, including the defence of a legal claim against the employer. This means that if an employee has brought a complaint against their employer to an employment tribunal, alleging for example that they have been subjected to race discrimination in the course of their employment, it would be legitimate for the employer to process information relating to the race or ethnic origin of that employee, and possibly the race or ethnic origin of other employees. This would be in order to facilitate the employer's defence against the claim, ie to prove to the tribunal's satisfaction that the employee alleging race discrimination had not in fact been treated less favourably than other employees in similar circumstances. Alternatively, if the employee had in fact been treated less favourably than another employee (for example if they had been unsuccessful in an application for a promotion), the employer would be entitled to produce sufficient evidence to persuade the tribunal that the reasons for the employer's actions (ie their selection of one employee in favour of another for promotion) had nothing to do with the respective racial groups of the respective employees.

Monitoring of job applicants and employees

8.10 Although there is no positive duty on employers to monitor their staff in terms of equality of opportunity (except in the public sector where there is a duty to monitor staff and job applicants by reference to their racial groups – see 8.13 below). Nevertheless monitoring is recognised as an appropriate tool for employers to use to ensure equality of opportunity within the organisation and to eliminate any discriminatory practices.

Monitoring for the purposes of promoting equal opportunities may be conducted on both job applicants and existing employees. Monitoring will essentially have three stages:

- gathering information about job applicants or employees;

- analysing and interpreting the information; and

- defining a programme of action to remedy any inequalities that have been identified.

Where monitoring is carried out, the employer will be under a duty to ensure the security of the personal data gathered. This is in line with the seventh data protection principle, namely that employers should put in place measures to protect personal data against unauthorised or unlawful processing, accidental loss or destruction, or damage. In order to achieve this goal, the employer should:

- limit the number of staff who have access to personal information obtained as a result of equal opportunities monitoring (and also other forms of monitoring);

- ensure staff who have access to personal data, and in particular sensitive data, have been fully trained so as to ensure that they understand their duties and obligations under the *DPA 1998* including the data protection principles; and

- refrain from using personal information collected for the purposes of equal opportunities monitoring for any other purpose.

Job applicants

8.11 It is considered good practice for organisations to carry out monitoring of job applications in order to promote equality of opportunity as between people of different racial groups, both sexes and all ages, and to protect against any inequalities that may otherwise creep into the recruitment process. The information is usually gathered on a separate, tear-off portion of the application form so that data such as an individual's ethnic origin is not used as part of the criteria for selection.

One of the key principles in the Employment Practices Code is that information should not be collected and retained about individuals unless it is necessary for a legitimate business purpose. Whilst monitoring of racial origin, gender, disability, age and possibly religion may be justified as part of the recruitment process to ensure equality of opportunity and the avoidance of discrimination, once the recruitment exercise is complete, the further retention of data relating to unsuccessful candidates is unlikely to be justifiable. Instead, the employer should devise a system for retaining anonymised data on the numbers of candidates who applied for each post and the number shortlisted, together with their 'categories' eg gender, family status, racial origin, age and whether or not they are disabled. In this way, the data is no longer 'personal data' for the purposes of the *DPA 1998*, but will still allow the employer to conduct a meaningful review of the figures.

Anonymised data will be sufficient to allow the employer to draw the necessary conclusions, ie whether the number of shortlisted applicants and successful applicants in each category (ie sex, racial group, etc) are proportionate to that category's numbers in the organisation, and within the community as a whole. The names of the individuals (or other identifying features such as serial numbers that can then be tracked back to an individual) will no longer be necessary for this purpose.

Existing employees

8.12 Before embarking on a process of monitoring existing employees, the employer should review the advice available from the Equality and Human Rights Commission (EHRC) at: www.equalityhumanrights.com.

It is good practice for employers to take specific advice about the monitoring forms, procedures and ethnic grouping categories to be used in any monitoring exercise. The range of choices of ethnic origin should not be limited to the extent that those completing the form are obliged to make a choice that does not properly reflect their ethnic origin.

Where an employee declines to complete a monitoring questionnaire, the employer should:

● keep a record of the fact that the employee did not complete the form; and

● if the employer elects to assign categories to employees who declined to complete the form, note that the categorisations have been made by the employer and not the employee, and that the categorisations are therefore based on assumption and not fact.

Public sector employers' duty to monitor in respect of racial groups

8.13 The *Race Relations Act 1976* prohibits discrimination on grounds of colour, race, nationality, ethnic origins and national origins. This Act applies throughout the process of recruitment, during employment, at termination of employment and post-employment (for example in respect of any reference provided to an ex-employee).

The *Race Relations (Amendment) Act 2000* imposed a general duty on all public authorities to take positive measures to eliminate unlawful racial discrimination and promote equality of opportunity and good relations as between persons of different racial groups. The *Race Relations Act 1976 (Statutory Duties) Order 2001 (SI 2001 No 3458)* obliged public sector organisations to prepare and publish a race equality scheme, ie a plan as to how they intend to achieve racial equality in their employment practices and to ensure the training of all staff on racial equality. Article 5(2) and (3) of the Order also imposed a duty on public sector employers to carry out regular monitoring of the racial balance of their employees and all applicants for employment, training and promotion.

Where a public sector employer has 150 or more full-time staff (or the equivalent, taking into account the hours worked by part-time staff), there are further duties on public sector employers to collect information relating to the racial groups of staff who:

- receive training;

- benefit or suffer detriment as a result of performance assessment procedures;

- are involved in grievance procedures;

- are the subject of disciplinary procedures; and

- cease employment.

The law requires the results of this monitoring to be published annually.

The imposition of this public duty means that public sector organisations can rely on the existence of the legal duty as a justification for retaining records associated with equal opportunities monitoring in respect of the racial groups of their employees and job applicants. As stated in 8.7 above, however, if the employer wishes also to monitor in respect of certain other features, for example religion or disability, employees' explicit consent will be required since the information being sought will constitute sensitive data under the *DPA 1998*.

Disability

8.14 Under the *Disability Discrimination Act 1995* (*DDA 1995*), all employers are obliged:

- not to treat a job applicant, employee or ex-employee unfavourably because the individual has a disability or (unless the particular treatment can be justified) on grounds related to their disability; and

- to make reasonable adjustments to their working arrangements, working practices and (where relevant) premises in order to accommodate the needs of the particular disabled person.

A disabled person is defined in the Act as someone who 'has a physical or mental impairment which has a substantial and long-term adverse effect on his ability to carry out normal day-to-day activities'. 'Long-term' in this context means 12 months or more. To qualify as a disabled person, the impairment must have a substantial adverse effect on one of the following:

- mobility;

- manual dexterity;

- physical coordination;

- continence;

- the ability to lift, carry or otherwise move everyday objects;

- speech, hearing or eyesight;

- memory or ability to concentrate, learn or understand; or

- the perception of the risk of physical danger.

Someone with a severe disfigurement will also be classed as disabled under the Act.

The *DDA 1995* is thus very wide in scope and covers:

- a range of physical illnesses, conditions and injuries;

- any mental illness or condition including many stress related ill-nesses;

- progressive conditions such as muscular dystrophy or Alzheimer's disease, which are covered as soon as the condition is diagnosed, provided there are some effects on the person's normal day-to-day activities at that point in time and these effects are likely to become substantial;

- multiple sclerosis, cancer and HIV, which are automatically regarded as disabilities from the point of diagnosis irrespective of the level of effect on the individual;

- recurring conditions, even during periods of remission, provided the condition is likely to recur;

- conditions that fluctuate between minor and substantial; and

- past disabilities.

The *DDA 1995* protects all workers and also job applicants. Like the other anti-discrimination statutes, it does not require an employee to have any minimum period of service in order to be eligible to bring a complaint to an employment tribunal. It places considerable responsibility on employers to be positive in their attitude to the employment of people with disabilities and to do whatever they reasonably can to accommodate their needs.

Apart from outlawing discrimination on grounds related to disability, the *DDA 1995* imposes a duty on employers to make reasonable adjustments to any 'provision, criterion or practice' applied by the employer which 'places the disabled person concerned at a substantial disadvantage' in comparison with people who are not disabled, in order to accommodate the needs of disabled workers and job applicants. The phrase 'provision, criterion or practice' can include a wide range of policies, procedures, criteria and conditions for appointment or promotion, requirements and conditions of the job and individual decisions affecting a disabled employee or job applicant. Failure to meet this duty will render employers liable to claims of disability discrimination.

There is, however, no general duty to make adjustments within the employment context, but instead the duty arises when an employee becomes disabled or someone with a disability applies for a job. Some examples of adjustments to working practices could be to:

- transfer the employee to a different job in circumstances where the employee is no longer able to perform their own job, bearing in mind that this could only be done lawfully with the employee's express agreement (an enforced transfer would be in breach of the employee's contract);

- alter the employee's job duties, or allocate some of the duties to another employee if, as a result of a disability, the employee cannot carry out those duties or has difficulty carrying them out;

- adjust how the job is done, for example by arranging for an employee with a mobility impairment to have work brought to their work station rather than requiring the person to walk to other parts of the building;

- adjust working hours, for example to fit in with the employee's need to attend weekly medical appointments, or by providing additional or longer rest breaks if the employee's condition causes them to tire easily;

- move an employee who uses a wheelchair to a different place of work, for example locate them somewhere more readily accessible;

- allow an employee whose disability means they cannot drive to work partly from home;

- acquire or modify equipment to assist a disabled person to perform their job (grants are often available);

- adjust procedural requirements, for example by condoning more frequent periods of absence from work than would normally be acceptable;

- modify instructions or manuals, for example by providing them on cassette tape, or in Braille;

- provide additional supervision or coaching, for example to assist an employee with learning difficulties to grasp the key principles of a new method of working;

- adjust selection tests for job applicants, for example by using a different method of testing for a candidate with dyslexia so that they are given the opportunity to compete for the job on a level playing field;

- modify premises, for example by installing a ramp, widening a doorway or moving furniture for a wheelchair user or relocating door handles or shelves for someone who has difficulty reaching.

The duty to make adjustments is subject to the word 'reasonable' and it will therefore not be necessary for an employer to make adjustments where, for example:

- making the adjustment would incur excessive cost in relation to the employer's size and resources;

- making the adjustment would be impracticable or would cause major disruption to the employer's business;

- the adjustment would not help the employee or would be unacceptable to them; or

- making the adjustment would contravene health and safety law, fire regulations or any other legislation.

As a result of the duties imposed under the *DDA 1995*, and in order to promote good practice generally, many employers conduct monitoring in respect of job applicants and employees with disabilities. Furthermore, as stated earlier, it will be necessary for an employer to collect and retain data about a disabled employee's condition and its effects if they are to be in a position to fulfil their obligation under the *DDA 1995* to make reasonable adjustments for that person.

The type of monitoring that may be undertaken could, for example, include tracking how many people with disabilities are being promoted within the organisation, and to what levels of seniority. This type of monitoring will require data to be kept on specific individuals in relation to promotions, and it will not be possible to hold the data anonymously. Employees would therefore have the right to be informed of the type of monitoring that was taking place and how their personal data was used as part of the monitoring process.

The collection and retention of data about an individual's state of health and about their disability should be the subject of open discussion between the employer and the disabled person. Disability should not be regarded as a taboo subject in the field of employment and in any event, it will arguably be necessary for the employer to raise the question of how the person's disability affects them in order to be able to determine what types of adjustments would assist them to perform the job. The disabled person will obviously have a more in-depth knowledge of what measures would be likely to help facilitate effective working and help them to overcome any disadvantage that their disability would otherwise cause. Thus the provision in the *DPA 1998, Schedule 3* that allows employers to process sensitive data if it is necessary to do so in order to comply with a legal obligation will be satisfied.

There is no duty in the *DDA 1995* on a job applicant or employee to reveal a disability, unless asked. The onus therefore lies with the employer to raise the issue, ask appropriate questions and make an appropriate record in order to establish what adjustments might reasonably be required for them to fulfil the duties imposed under the *DDA 1995*.

Recommendations of the Employment Practices Code in relation to equal opportunities monitoring

8.15 Part 2 of the Employment Practices Code contains a section on equal opportunities monitoring which expressly recommends that employers should:

- make sure that the processing of information about employees' racial and ethnic origin, religion, sexual orientation and/or disability satisfies one of the conditions for the processing of sensitive data (see 8.6 above);

- collect information that identifies individual employees only where it is necessary in order to conduct meaningful equal opportunities monitoring;

- keep information relevant to monitoring in an anonymised form if possible;

- ensure that any information gathered for monitoring purposes that identifies individuals is not used for any other purpose; and

- ensure that the questions on monitoring forms are designed so that they will collect information that is accurate and not excessive.

The Code of Practice is not legally binding, but represents the Information Commissioner's recommendations as to how employers should fulfil their legal requirements under the *DPA 1998* in relation to the collection and use of personal information relating to job applicants and employees. Even though there is no legal duty to follow the Code's recommendations, a court or tribunal can, in the event of a legal challenge against the employer, take the provisions of the Code into account. This means that if there is evidence that the employer has declined or failed to comply with the provisions of the Code, the chances of a court or tribunal making a finding against them will be substantially increased.

Equal pay questionnaires

8.16 In April 2003, a procedure was introduced to allow employees to serve a questionnaire on their employer requesting information about their pay in comparison to someone of the opposite sex doing similar work. This was introduced through the *Equal Pay (Questions and Replies) Order 2003 (SI 2003 No 722)* made under the *Employment Act 2002*. The key aim of the questionnaire procedure is to speed up the resolution of equal pay disputes by allowing the potential claimant to gain useful information at an early stage. An employee may use this procedure either before commencing equal pay proceedings in an employment tribunal (for example to allow a decision to be made on whether or not such a claim would have any merit), or after such proceedings have already been instigated.

Similar procedures are in place in respect of complaints under the other discrimination laws, allowing employees to question their employer about alleged discriminatory treatment on grounds of sex, race, religion or belief, sexual orientation, age and disability.

The *Equal Pay Act 1970 (EPA 1970)* covers equality of treatment in pay and contractual terms as between men and women – where a man and a woman are doing like work, work rated as equivalent (in a job evaluation scheme) or work of equal value. Although men and women are equally protected under the *EPA 1970*, in practice most claims are brought by women.

How to answer an employee's questions without breaching the DPA 1998

8.17 Because the type of information that an individual may seek under the equal pay questionnaire procedure usually involves personal data relating to another employee, or several other employees, the *DPA 1998* is a relevant feature of this process. This compels employers to balance their duties under the Act against the rights of the employee under the statutory procedure to request information about the employer's pay practices in order that they can satisfy themselves that they are not being subjected to sex discrimination.

The purpose of the equal pay questionnaire

8.18 The key purpose of the equal pay questionnaire is to assist employees to obtain relevant information where they believe that their level of pay is unjustifiably less than a comparator of the opposite sex who is performing work at the same level. The information, if provided, will enable the employee to establish whether or not they are receiving equal pay and, if not, the reasons for any differences or discrepancies. The provision of clear information from the employer may, arguably, satisfy the employee that the reason for any difference in respect of pay and benefits is unconnected with gender, and thus stop a claim for equal pay going forward to a tribunal.

Legal effect of the equal pay questionnaire

8.19   As stated at 8.16 above, an employee who is bringing, or considering bringing, an equal pay claim against their employer can elect to serve an equal pay questionnaire on the employer. There is, however, no statutory obligation on the employer to respond to an equal pay questionnaire served upon them, but because the replies given (or lack of them) are admissible in evidence, a failure to reply can be taken into account by an employment tribunal if an equal pay claim is taken forward. Essentially, the employer will place themselves at a disadvantage if, at a subsequent tribunal claim for equal pay, the evidence shows that they declined without good reason to answer the employee's questions, provided incomplete answers, or gave answers that were equivocal, evasive or untrue. This would be likely to lead the tribunal into drawing inferences that were unfavourable to the employer. It is therefore in employers' interests to ensure they provide a carefully worded and detailed response to the employee's questions. The time limit for doing so is eight weeks.

The equal pay questionnaire form

8.20   The form (which is available in a pre-printed version) includes factual questions to establish whether the employee is receiving less pay than a named comparator, and if so, why. The named comparator(s) must be someone whom the employee believes is performing like work or work of equal value. The questionnaire includes:

- space for the employee to identify a comparator (or more than one comparator), ie the employee(s) of the opposite sex whom the employee believes are engaged on like work or work of equal value;

- space for the employee to state why they believe they are not receiving equal pay in relation to the named comparator(s);

- a question asking the employer whether they agree that the named comparator(s) is/are engaged on like work or work of equal value;

- questions to establish whether the employee is in fact receiving less pay than the named comparator(s) and if so, why.

The form also includes space for the employee to add their own questions, which allows individuals to tailor the form to their own specific situation. Questions may, for example, be asked about how pay is determined, how skills and experience are reflected in the employer's pay system, any job grading scheme in operation and specific information about the named comparator's pay and benefits package.

Data protection issues associated with equal pay questionnaires

8.21   Whenever an equal pay questionnaire is served on an employer, there will inevitably be data protection and confidentiality issues to take into account. Information as to details of employees' pay will constitute personal data for the purposes of the *DPA 1998*, although pay does not fall into the category of 'sensitive data'.

One of the most obvious problems for the employer is that it may be viewed as inappropriate to disclose to the employee who has served the questionnaire how much another employee is earning, what benefits package they have under their contract of employment or how they were assessed under a recent appraisal review that was linked to a pay rise.

One key point to bear in mind, however is that there is nothing in the Act that expressly prevents the disclosure of employees' salaries for the purpose of responding to an equal pay questionnaire. Pay is not classed as 'sensitive data' and hence not subject to the restrictive provisions in place to protect such data (see 8.5 above). Furthermore, the *DPA 1998, section 35* states that personal data will be 'exempt from the non-disclosure provisions where the disclosure is necessary for the purpose of, or in connection with, any legal proceedings (including prospective legal proceedings). Where an employee has served an equal pay questionnaire on the employer, this will indicate that either legal proceedings under the *Equal Pay Act 1970* have been instigated, or that the employee is thinking about commencing such proceedings, thus falling squarely within the meaning of *section 35*.

In any event, there is nothing to stop an employer who is concerned about the disclosure of pay information from consulting the named comparator in relation to the proposed disclosure of their pay to the employee who has served the questionnaire. The employer can explain to the employee that it is necessary in the interests of justice for them to disclose details of their pay and benefits package to the person who has served the questionnaire. It may be that an employee will have no objection to the potential disclosure of this information to a colleague, and even if they do object, they may understand why it is necessary in the interests of justice for the employer to make the disclosure. Permitting an employee to refuse to consent to the disclosure of the requisite information could cause considerable disgruntlement to the employee who served the equal pay questionnaire, thus increasing the chances that a claim for equal pay could be taken to an employment tribunal. Given the statutory force of the equal pay questionnaire procedure, a tribunal may not regard the employee's unwillingness to agree to the disclosure as a legitimate reason for the employer to decline to disclose the relevant information.

Arguably, therefore, the disclosure of an employee's pay in response to the serving of an equal pay questionnaire is necessary if justice is to be achieved, unless of course the employee's questions are obviously frivolous or misconceived, in which case the employer would be justified in refusing to disclose the information requested on those grounds.

Providing generalised information

8.22 Concerns over confidentiality and data protection will not, however genuine, excuse the employer from providing a response to the employee who has submitted an equal pay questionnaire. It is likely that in many cases information can be readily provided about a number of items that do not constitute personal data under the Act, for example information about:

- the employer's general pay structures and how pay is determined;

- any job evaluation scheme in place within the organisation;

- how skills and experience are reflected in the pay system or job evaluation scheme;

- pay grades or bandings;

- the minimum and maximum pay for each grade or band;

- the average salary of a group of employees who are performing the same work as the employee who submitted the questionnaire;

- criteria that the employer uses to determine individual pay rises;

- the fact that another employee is, or is not, receiving a higher rate of pay than the person submitting the questionnaire (without disclosing the actual amount of the employee's pay);

- how the employee's own salary and recent pay rises have been determined;

- the reasons why the employee's pay is set at its current level; and

- whether the employer has an equal opportunities policy in place and what the policy says in relation to pay.

Disclosing the types of information listed above will not compromise the anonymity or confidence of individual employees. Furthermore, if the employee has named several comparators, rather than just one, the employer may be able to disclose an average of their salaries, thus avoiding any possibility of a breach of confidence.

The employer can also, if appropriate, give an explanation of any significant differences between the job duties of the person serving the questionnaire and those of their chosen comparator, ie any factors that justify a difference in pay. There may also be other genuine, non sex-based reasons for a difference in pay, for example a difference in the level of qualifications or type of experience as between the employee and their chosen comparator. The employer may be able to make a general statement to this effect without disclosing precise details about the comparator's background.

In general, the employer should provide as much information as they reasonably can in response to an employee's equal pay questionnaire, in particular where the data can be anonymised thus allowing meaningful information to be disclosed whilst also preserving the confidentiality of other employees' pay and benefits packages.

Court orders in relation to the disclosure of information

8.23 It is worth bearing in mind that, even where an employer has refused to disclose information on the grounds that it is confidential, an employee who pursues a claim through an employment tribunal can ask the tribunal to order the employer to disclose the relevant information for the purpose of dealing with the claim. The tribunal will order disclosure if they believe that it is in the interests of justice to do so. The *DPA 1998, section 35* states that personal data will be 'exempt from the non-disclosure provisions where the disclosure is required by or under any enactment, by any rule of law or by the order of a court'.

Further information about equal pay questionnaires is available in the Equal Opportunities Commission's Code of Practice on Equal Pay, available from www.equalityhumanrights.com.

Chapter 9   Employee monitoring

Introduction

9.1   Monitoring the activities of people at work is an important but sensitive issue. Clearly no reasonable employer would wish to intrude unnecessarily into employees' private lives, nor alienate their staff. Nevertheless, it can be argued that a degree of monitoring of employees at work is a business necessity for many employers in order to protect their interests, together with those of their staff and their clients. The main aim should be to strike a reasonable balance between the need to monitor as judged against employees' rights in contract, including the mutual duty of trust and confidence, and the right to privacy under the *Human Rights Act 1998* (*HRA 1998*). Essentially, monitoring should be carried out only where it is necessary and relevant to the business, and where the legitimate business needs of the employer outweigh the inevitable intrusion into employees' private lives.

Before deciding what type of monitoring to carry out and how the monitoring is to be targeted, the employer may wish to consider the legal issues relating to restrictions on employee monitoring and weigh these up against the legal risks of not monitoring. Arguably, most employees will be capable of understanding the need for a reasonable degree of monitoring, provided that managers clearly explain the employer's position and the reasons why monitoring is necessary for the organisation.

The key objective of this chapter is to explore the data protection implications of monitoring employees at work, in particular with regard to monitoring employees' use of the telephone, email and the internet. Equal opportunities monitoring is dealt with in CHAPTER 8.

What is employee monitoring?

9.2   Part 3 of the Employment Practices Code (Monitoring at Work) (see 9.10 below) defines monitoring as any activity that is designed to 'collect information about workers by keeping them under some form of observation, normally with a view to checking their performance or conduct'. Both the Code and the accompanying Supplementary Guidance contain a great deal of useful information for employers on the subject of monitoring employees' activities at work.

The *Data Protection Act 1998* (*DPA 1998* or 'the Act') and Part 3 of the Code of Practice will be engaged only if a record is kept of the employer's monitoring activities. If, for example, a manager listens in to an employee's telephone calls, but does not create any record of the calls nor of the fact they were monitored, then there will be no 'personal data' to protect. By contrast, if the manager was to make a written note of (for example) the employee's name and a summary of the content of the calls, then a record will have been created, thus potentially giving rise to issues under the Act and the Code of Practice (depending on how the written record is subsequently retained).

Whose records are protected?

9.3 Employers will need to consider records they hold about:

- their current employees, including temporary and part-time employees;
- agency staff;
- casual workers;
- contract staff;
- apprentices;
- students who work for the organisation;
- anyone on a work experience placement with the organisation;
- past employees, so long as the record identifies the ex-employee;
- job applicants (whether successful or unsuccessful);
- their customers and clients;
- suppliers; and
- anyone else where the record identifies an individual.

The purpose of monitoring

9.4 There may be many different reasons why an employer may legitimately decide to monitor the activities of their employees. The main purposes of monitoring are likely to be to (the points below are not in any particular order):

- obtain information about employees' efficiency and productivity;
- ensure quality of the employer's product or service;

- check whether there is any evidence of malpractice on the part of workers generally, or by a particular worker;

- protect the employer against legal liability, for example in the event of inappropriate use or serious misuse of email or the internet;

- record information as part of employees' training;

- maintain records in case of a customer complaint;

- ensure security measures are effective; and

- ensure that safety policies and procedures are being implemented properly in order to protect employees working in a hazardous environment.

Part 3 of the Employment Practices Code (on Monitoring at Work – see 9.10 below) recommends that employers should not be tempted to monitor their workers just because one of their customers or clients has imposed a condition requiring them to carry out such monitoring. Instead, the employer should carry out an impact assessment (see 9.11 below) to review whether monitoring is justifiable in the circumstances. The Code points out that a condition of business imposed by a customer cannot override the employer's responsibilities under the Act.

The potential benefits of monitoring

9.5 Monitoring should be carried out only where the employer is clear about the purpose(s) of the monitoring, and where they have clearly established that the type of monitoring that is proposed will bring tangible benefits to the organisation. Benefits could include:

- a reduction in the likelihood that employees will misuse the employer's computer and telephone systems;

- protection against legal action that might be taken by employees against the employer on account of any alleged breach of their employment rights; and

- an increase in quality, efficiency and productivity.

Responsibility for monitoring

9.6 It is important for all employers to identify who within their organisation will be responsible for employee monitoring, and for ensuring that employment policies and procedures on monitoring comply with legislation, including the *DPA 1998*.

The person appointed to hold such responsibility should, ideally, be a senior manager who has sufficient authority to challenge any practices that might risk being in breach of legislation or associated Codes of Practice and make decisions about data protection compliance. In a large organisation, a senior HR manager would be an ideal candidate for such responsibility, whilst in a small business it may be appropriate for the owner or managing director to hold responsibility. Alternatively, the Company Secretary could be charged with responsibility for data protection matters.

Whichever senior manager is appointed, that person should be responsible for ensuring policies and procedures are regularly checked, in particular against the *DPA 1998* and the Employment Practices Code. The manager should also be made accountable for ensuring that policies and procedures are put into practice by all staff, and especially by those whose jobs take them into contact with personal data held about employees. Particular examples include line managers and supervisors, and HR or IT staff who may be involved in the processes of monitoring, and who may consequently gain access to a range of information about other staff in the course of their work.

Someone who is newly appointed to the role that involves responsibility for monitoring may wish to review:

- what personal data about employees exists within the organisation and where and by whom it is held;

- the type of information produced by monitoring and whether it is genuinely appropriate to the needs of the organisation;

- whether any information obtained through monitoring is unnecessary and whether the employer should consequently refrain from collecting it (or discard it);

- whether it is necessary or appropriate for individuals other than HR staff to hold personal data about staff, especially information gleaned from monitoring;

- whether any sensitive data is likely to be obtained as a result of monitoring, and if so whether one of the conditions for the processing of sensitive data is satisfied;

- whether clear data protection guidelines have been devised and communicated to all staff involved in monitoring;

- whether newly recruited staff are properly informed of the employer's data protection rules and guidelines during induction;

- whether those who have access to personal data are aware of their legal responsibilities under the *DPA 1998* and that they may be held personally liable for any breach of the Act.

Different forms of monitoring

9.7   Monitoring can take many forms and can include:

- the interception of employees' telephone calls, voicemails or email messages, where a record is subsequently created;

- checking logs of telephone numbers called by employees, whether individually or by group;

- using automated software to collect information about the types of emails employees are sending or receiving;

- creating a log of the internet sites visited by employees, whether by individual or as a group;

- keeping recordings of telephone calls made to or from a call centre;

- CCTV or audio surveillance;

- videoing workers outside the workplace;

- installing devices into company vehicles to track the location of the vehicle;

- supervisory observation;

- checking up on employees through credit reference agencies or the Criminal Records Bureau (or Disclosure Scotland); and

- gathering information through point-of-sale terminals in order to check the efficiency of individuals who are employed as check-out operators, for example in a supermarket.

Whenever a record is created about any of the above activities in which one or more individuals can be identified, the DPA 1998 will be activated.

Covert monitoring

9.8   Covert monitoring should not normally be undertaken within the workplace. 'Covert monitoring' is defined in the Employment Practices Code as 'monitoring carried out in a manner calculated to ensure those subject to it are unaware that it is taking place'. The only exception to the general principle that covert monitoring should not be carried out in employment would be in circumstances where there were proper grounds for suspecting an employee of criminal activity or equivalent malpractice (for example a suspected serious breach of safety rules), and it was reasonable to conclude that informing the employee that they were to be monitored would prejudice prevention or detection of the malpractice. If in doubt about whether to instigate covert monitoring, the employer should consider whether the criminal activity of which the employee is suspected is one that would be sufficiently serious to justify involving the police (although the decision as to whether to involve the police will, of course, be a separate decision that management will be entitled to make for themselves). If the answer to that question is 'yes', then covert monitoring may be justified, depending on all the circumstances.

The Code of Practice suggests that any covert monitoring to be carried out should normally be authorised by senior management and the accompanying Guidance recommends that the employer should limit the number of staff involved in any covert monitoring and set down very clear rules restricting the access to and disclosure of any personal information obtained as a result.

The Code also recommends that, in circumstances where covert monitoring is justified, the employer should take steps to ensure that any incidental information gathered about the employee that has nothing to do with their suspected wrongdoing is disregarded and subsequently deleted from the employee's file.

Dealing with information obtained from monitoring

9.9 Information gained as a result of monitoring must be treated in accordance with the provisions of the Act and the Employment Practices Code. The Code suggests that, where information gathered as a result of monitoring might have an adverse impact on an employee, the information should be presented to the employee to allow them to comment on it and make representations. This should be done before any decision is taken as to whether there are grounds for disciplinary action against the employee. It is noted in the Code that equipment and systems sometimes malfunction, resulting in the possibility of inaccurate or misleading information being produced. There is the further possibility of information being misinterpreted. Employees should always be given a full and fair opportunity to comment on, challenge or explain the results of any monitoring exercise whenever the results may be detrimental to them.

The Employment Practices Code and monitoring

9.10 The Employment Practices Code, Part 3 (Monitoring at Work) is available at: www.ico.gov.uk. The Code represents the Information Commissioner's interpretation of how the *DPA 1998* should be implemented with regard to monitoring the activities of employees at work. Useful Supplementary Guidance accompanies the Code. The Code does not prevent monitoring of employees at work, but rather sets out to regulate when and how monitoring is carried out.

The Code, like other Codes of Practice, is not legally binding on employers, but a failure to follow its recommendations can be used in evidence against an employer in the event of a court or tribunal claim. It is therefore in employers' interests to follow the Code, which in any event is a useful source of information and guidance.

In general, information will be covered by the Act and the Code of Practice if an individual can be identified (whether by name or by other means, for example a reference number). The *DPA 1998* covers:

- information held manually, whether (for example) in a structured filing system, a reference card system or in a supervisor's notebook;

- information held on computer; and

- information contained in the body of an email.

Where, however, information is held about a group of people in such a way that individuals are not named or otherwise identifiable, the information will not constitute personal data, and hence will not be covered by either the Act or the Code of Practice.

Impact assessments

9.11 One of the key recommendations of the Code of Practice is that employers should carry out an impact assessment in order to decide whether monitoring is appropriate for their business, and determine how any monitoring should be carried out. Through the impact assessment, the employer should review the likely effect of monitoring on the privacy and other rights of employees, and establish whether or not any adverse impact of monitoring on employees is justifiable when balanced against the needs of the employer (see 9.13 below). Impact assessments should be conducted to establish justification for monitoring in a general sense and also to review whether or not monitoring in specific circumstances would be justifiable (see 9.15 below).

The Code explains that an impact assessment involves:

- identifying the purpose(s) of any proposed monitoring and its likely benefits;

- identifying any likely adverse impact on employees of monitoring, for example the inevitable intrusion into employees' private lives that monitoring will cause (see 9.13 below);

- considering alternatives to monitoring or different ways in which monitoring might be carried out (see 9.17 below);

- taking into account the obligations that arise out of monitoring; and

- deciding whether or not monitoring is justified (see 9.15 below).

The benefits of carrying out an impact assessment

9.12 There may, in any event, be considerable benefits for the employer in conducting a written impact assessment with regard to employee monitoring, for example:

- conducting an impact assessment in an open and transparent manner will create trust between management and staff and hence enhance employee relations generally;

- the results of the assessment will help employees to understand why certain forms of monitoring are necessary for the organisation;

- the assessment should assist employees' general understanding of data protection issues and the parameters of workplace privacy;

- the measured and targeted approach required to conduct an impact assessment will ultimately save the employer time and resources; and

- if at any time legal action is taken against the employer in relation to workplace monitoring, the fact that the employer has conducted an impact assessment will place them in a much stronger position to defend the action.

Adverse impact

9.13 Monitoring at work will inevitably have some adverse impact on employees. Part 3 of the Employment Practices Code suggests that an impact assessment should be carried out in relation to proposed monitoring (see 9.11 above) and that one of the purposes of this will be for the employer to identify the likely extent of any adverse impact that monitoring would create for employees (or for others, for example customers or suppliers).

The first and most obvious general adverse consequence of monitoring will be the inevitable intrusion into employees' private lives that monitoring will cause. It has been accepted in law that the right to respect for privacy (under *Article 8* of the *HRA 1998*) extends into the workplace (see 9.38–9.39 below). Some employees may resent the very idea of monitoring in principle, whilst others may fear its effects or suspect management of underhand dealings. Excessive monitoring, or monitoring without proper cause, could also be perceived as a breach of the employer's duty of trust and confidence towards their employees and, in a worst scenario, could lead to an employee resigning and complaining to an employment tribunal that their treatment amounted to unfair constructive dismissal.

These concerns can, to a great extent, be resolved, or at least minimised, by regular open two-way communication between management and staff and by making all monitoring policies and procedures transparent and ensuring they are well regulated. Arguably, most employees will be capable of understanding the need for a reasonable degree of monitoring, provided that managers clearly explain the employer's position and the reasons why monitoring is necessary for the organisation.

Minimising the intrusion into employees' privacy

9.14 The employer should take steps to minimise the intrusion into employee's privacy by:

- providing a transparent system of monitoring and a procedure that allows employees to be aware when monitoring that might affect them is being carried out;

- ensuring that the type of monitoring carried out is not any more intrusive than is absolutely necessary to meet the employer's stated business objectives;

- restrict the numbers of staff involved in monitoring so as to limit the disclosure of any sensitive information about an individual that may come to light as a result of monitoring;

- avoid opening and reading emails whenever possible, especially those that are obviously personal or private, unless there is a clearly identifiable reason why it is necessary to examine the content of the email in question;

- devise systems and procedures that allow employees to communicate confidentially with certain professionals, ie so that staff know that certain types of communications will not be monitored. Examples would include employee communications with an occupational health practitioner, a counsellor whose services are provided by the employer, and a trade union representative.

Justification for monitoring

9.15 One of the key purposes of carrying out an impact assessment (see 9.11 above) will be so that the employer can determine whether or not any form of monitoring is justified. It should not be assumed that there is a business case for monitoring, but instead the employer should adopt an open-minded approach and examine:

- what the purposes of monitoring would be;

- whether the type of monitoring proposed might reasonably achieve those purposes;

- whether the results of the monitoring would produce benefits for the business that outweighed any adverse impact caused to employees;

- whether there is any alternative to monitoring that would be less intrusive to employees (see 9.17 below);

- whether the proposed systems of monitoring are fair towards staff in a general sense; and

- whether there has been a full process of consultation with trade unions, with employee representatives or with employees directly.

Assessing what type of monitoring is appropriate for the business

9.16 The Employment Practices Code makes it clear that proportionality is the key to compliance with the *DPA 1998,* ie the employer must design systems of monitoring that are linked to specific business needs and balance those needs against the reasonable rights of employees to be granted respect for their private lives and correspondence.

Employers who decide that it is prudent to carry out monitoring on their employees' use of the telephone, email and the internet will have to decide as a preliminary, but very important, issue whether monitoring should consist of:

- occasional spot-checks on the telephone numbers, email addresses and internet sites that are being accessed by employees generally, without pinpointing which employees are responsible for accessing specific numbers and sites; or

- specific checks on individual employees' use of the communications network by reviewing each person's access to telephone numbers, email addresses and internet sites individually. Often this would be done following the identification of a problem as a result of a general spot check, or following a complaint about a particular employee's activities; or

- interception of employees' telephone calls and email messages, ie listening to the calls and reading the email messages.

The important thing is to understand that, whenever a record is created of the communications that have been monitored, the provisions of the Act and the Employment Practices Code will be engaged. For example, where the employer records a telephone conversation, or creates a file on a particular employee's email and internet activities, the record would then be subject to the provisions of the Act and the Code and the data protection principles would have to be observed.

One key message inherent in the Code is that, if there is a less intrusive method for an employer to establish facts that they need to know, then they should pursue that less intrusive method (see 9.17 below). The only exception would be where the employer had reasonable grounds to suspect that an employee had been involved in criminal activity such as accessing child pornography on the internet, or serious misconduct, for example harassing another employee by email, or acting in breach of safety rules.

Alternatives to monitoring

9.17 The Code of Practice and its accompanying supplementary guidance stress that employers should consider alternatives to monitoring and cites as examples new methods of supervision or further training. The underlying message is that if there is an alternative, less intrusive, way of dealing with a particular situation, then monitoring should not be undertaken. The Code and Guidance also suggest that employers should seek to restrict monitoring, by:

- targeting monitoring only at employees who work in jobs which pose a particularly high risk to the employer, rather than monitoring everyone;

- monitoring only workers about whom complaints have been made, or about whom there are reasonable grounds to suspect misconduct;

- conducting spot-checks rather than continuous monitoring;

- adopting a policy of analysing email traffic rather than monitoring the content of messages, or reviewing whether traffic records can be used to narrow the scope of content monitoring;

- using technology that prevents misuse (such as web-filtering software) rather than introducing systems designed to detect misuse after the event;

- considering whether monitoring can be automated so that the information will be 'seen' only by a machine rather than by people.

The implications of monitoring employees' communications

9.18 Part 3 of the Employment Practices Code highlights the threat monitoring can pose to personal privacy and provides guidance on how employers can balance the requirement to protect employees' privacy against the need to pursue legitimate business interests.

In relation to monitoring of employees' email, telephone and internet use, the Code of Practice and supplementary guidance provide a number of suggestions for employers to:

- establish a policy (see 9.41 below) on the use of electronic communications that makes it clear whether, and if so to what extent, employees may use the employer's communications systems (telephone, laptop, mobile, fax, email, internet access) for personal or private communications;

- refrain from reading emails that are clearly personal or private and, if personal use of the email system is banned, consider instead whether sufficient information is available in the subject header or address of a particular email to instigate appropriate action against the employee for breach of the rules;

- provide secure lines of communication for employees so that they can transmit legitimate personal or sensitive information, for example to an occupational health adviser or a trade union official, in the knowledge that it will not be monitored;

- set up a system (where a reasonable level of personal use is permitted) whereby private emails can be marked 'personal and private' and adopt a policy of not monitoring such emails unless the employee is genuinely suspected of serious wrongdoing;

- if emails and/or voicemails need to be checked for incoming business messages when employees are away from work, make sure employees are informed that this may happen;

- inform all employees of the extent to which information about their email use and internet access is retained in the employer's system and for how long it is retained;

- consider whether it is sufficient to record the time employees spend accessing the internet rather than monitoring the actual sites visited or the content viewed.

In essence, the Code recommends that emails that are clearly personal or private should not be intercepted, even in organisations that impose a complete ban on personal use of email and the internet. The supplementary guidance to the Code points out that although a ban is an important factor, it is not necessarily an overriding one and the employer would have to be able to justify taking action to read a personal email by weighing up the intrusion into the employee's private life with the employer's need to know the content of the email. Some apparently personal emails may in any event be legitimate work-related messages, for example an email from an employee to an occupational health adviser concerning a personal health matter.

The inter-relationship between Data Protection Rules and the Lawful Business Practice Regulations 2000

9.19 The *Telecommunications* (*Lawful Business Practice*) (*Interception of Communications*) *Regulations 2000* (*SI 2000 No 2699*) (*LBP Regulations 2000*) make it lawful for an employer to monitor employees' communications provided monitoring is being done for one of the purposes specified in the Regulations. Under the *LBP Regulations 2000*, interception of employees' communications will be lawful provided it is carried out for one of the purposes listed at 9.25 below, and provided that the employer has taken all reasonable steps to inform employees and the people with whom they communicate that interception might take place. Employers are not required to gain employees' consent to monitoring if the purpose of the monitoring is consistent with one of the purposes approved in the Regulations, although they must ensure that employees are informed in advance of any monitoring that may take place. This contrasts with the general rule that interception without consent is against the law, ie the Regulations specify legitimate exceptions to the principle that consent to interception is required.

The *LBP Regulations 2000* are thus concerned with the question of whether the interception of employees' communications will be lawful, whilst the *DPA 1998* deals with the processing of information about employees. In respect of the information gathered as a result of interception, the Act will kick in whenever personal information about an individual is recorded and held on file, whether manually or on the employer's computer system.

Part 3 of the Employment Practices Code goes much further than the *LBP Regulations 2000* to protect employees from over-intrusive monitoring. Whilst the Regulations are concerned primarily with the purpose of monitoring and ensuring that employees are properly informed of their employer's monitoring policies and practices, the Code of Practice is concerned also with whether any data held on record as a result of monitoring is processed in accordance with the data protection principles.

The impact of the data protection principles on the operation of the LBP Regulations 2000

9.20 When taking steps to adhere to the *LBP Regulations 2000*, employers need also to bear in mind the eight data protection principles that form part of the *DPA 1998*. The first three data protection principles are particularly relevant, namely the duty to process personal data fairly and lawfully (see 9.21 below); the duty to obtain personal data only for one or more specified and lawful purposes (see 9.23 below); and the duty to ensure personal data are adequate, relevant and not excessive in relation to the purpose(s) for which they are processed (see 9.24 below).

The impact of the first data protection principle – processing personal data fairly and lawfully

9.21 The first data protection principle contained in the *DPA 1998, Schedule 1* creates the obligation on employers to process personal data 'fairly and lawfully' (see also 2.2 above). Where an employee has consented to monitoring, or if the monitoring is being conducted for one of the purposes authorised by the *LBP Regulations 2000* (see 9.25 below), it will be lawful. Fairness, however, is quite another matter. It is possible for monitoring to be lawful, but unfair. If, for example, an employer was to intercept and keep records of employees' personal emails (as opposed to work related emails) ostensibly for the purpose of investigating or detecting unauthorised use of the system (one of the permitted purposes available in the *LBP Regulations 2000*), this would be lawful, but could be unfair if such monitoring was excessive or carried out without good cause.

The duty under the Act to process personal data fairly and lawfully is subject to the proviso (contained in *Schedule 2* of the Act) that personal data must not be processed unless one of a number of conditions is fulfilled. The conditions are that:

- the employee has given their consent to the processing; or

- data processing is necessary for one of the following reasons:

    – for the performance of a contract, for example the processing of employees' wages;

    – in order to ensure compliance with a legal obligation, for example information about an employee's working hours may be necessary in order to comply with the *Working Time Regulations 1998 (SI 1998 No 1833)*;

    – to protect the vital interests of the employee;

    – for the administration of justice or for the exercise of any public functions;

    – for the purposes of legitimate interests pursued by the employer, for example if the business was about to be transferred.

It is important to note the word 'necessary' used in this part of the Act. If the employee's consent has not been obtained, data about that person can be processed only if one of the relevant conditions is necessary for the business, and not just because (for example) management would find it convenient.

This raises the interesting question of whether random monitoring of employees' email and internet use could be viewed as 'necessary' under the banner of 'performance of the contract'. It is highly unlikely that an employer would be able to assert in a general sense that monitoring of all employees' emails on a regular basis was necessary for the performance of employees' contracts. However, it may (arguably) be necessary to monitor an individual employee's emails or internet traffic following a specific complaint about that employee, or where there were reasonable grounds to suspect that the employee had been abusing the system. This acts as a reminder of the general principle inherent in the Act that monitoring of employees' communications should only take place if it is proportionate in light of the employer's legitimate business aims.

Obtaining employees' consent

9.22 On the face of it, it would appear that the most straightforward way of ensuring fairness in data processing is to obtain employees' consent to data processing, for example by including a clause authorising monitoring and recording of employees' communications in all employees' contracts of employment. Whilst obtaining employee consent to the monitoring and recording of data is advisable in a general sense, it is questionable whether this alone will act to protect the employer against a challenge of unfairness under the first data protection principle (the duty to process personal data fairly and lawfully). This is because the Employment Practices Code points out that there are limitations as to how far consent can be relied on in an employment context to justify the processing of personal data generally. This is because consent must be 'freely given' in order for it to be valid under the *DPA 1998*. In an employment relationship, the balance of power is not even and it may be that an employee feels that they have no choice but to agree to sign a document giving their consent. The Code stresses that a better way forward for employers is to conduct a proper impact assessment (see 9.11 above), rather than rely on employee consent to authorise monitoring and data recording.

This does not, however, mean that seeking employee consent should be dispensed with. It is still advisable to request each employee's consent to both monitoring and recording, whilst at the same time clearly informing the employee about the purpose for which the data obtained from monitoring will be used, who in the organisation will have access to the data, and any other relevant information. The key to fairness in processing is transparency.

The duty to obtain and process personal data only for specified and lawful purposes

9.23 The second data protection principle (*DPA 1998, Schedule 1*) is the duty to obtain and process personal data only for one or more specified and lawful purposes, and not process it in any manner incompatible with those purposes (see also 2.3 above). This means that employers must specify clearly the purpose(s) for which they intend to obtain and process data about employees. It would be unlawful therefore for an employer to use information obtained from monitoring for any purpose other than that defined as the purpose of the monitoring. This restriction would appear to prevent employers from using information about an employee that is uncovered by chance as a result of monitoring for other purposes.

The duty to ensure that personal data is adequate, relevant and not excessive

9.24 The third data protection principle cited in the *DPA 1998, Schedule 1* imposes a duty on employers to ensure that personal data is adequate, relevant and not excessive in relation to the data's stated purpose or purposes (see also 2.4 above). This means that employers should ensure that any personal information they hold about their employees is created and stored for a proper business purpose, and that, in relation to this purpose, the information is relevant, sufficient, and not excessive.

This could be interpreted as a requirement for employers to use the least intrusive means possible to achieve their business aims, a principle that is put forward also in Part 3 of the Employment Practices Code (see 9.10 above). It may, for example, be excessive or irrelevant in relation to an employer's business to monitor all employees' emails on a routine basis, where spot monitoring, or monitoring of selected employees' correspondence, would suffice to protect the interests of the business.

The circumstances in which it is lawful for an employer to monitor employees' communications under the LBP Regulations 2000

9.25 Under the *LBP Regulations 2000*, it will be lawful for an employer to intercept and record an employee's email correspondence and telephone calls and/or monitor internet use in the circumstances listed at 9.26 to 9.34 below, irrespective of whether or not the employee has given their express consent to the interception. The employee must, however, have been informed that interception may take place (see 9.19 above).

To establish the existence of facts relevant to the business

9.26 It may be justifiable for an employer to intercept and record employees' telephone calls or email messages in circumstances where the business transactions of the organisation are conducted largely by telephone or email. The employer may, for example, legitimately wish to maintain records to provide evidence about the terms of contracts they have entered into or details of other business transactions.

To ascertain compliance with regulatory and self-regulatory practices or procedures that are relevant to the business

9.27 This heading is potentially very wide in scope. Whenever an organisation seeks to monitor in order to achieve compliance with any Regulations, Codes of Practice or Guidance issued by bodies such as DBERR, ACAS, the Equality and Human Rights Commission or the Health and Safety Executive (for example), monitoring would be potentially legitimate. Equally, potentially anything issued by any EU-based organisation that had amongst its objectives the publication of Codes of Practice or Standards could give rise to a legitimate decision to monitor employee communications.

To ascertain or demonstrate standards that employees achieve or ought to achieve when using the employer's systems of communication

9.28 This clause allows employers to monitor and record employees' communications for the purpose of ensuring that the organisation's quality standards (for example standards of customer care) are being met, or to demonstrate standards that should be met as part of a training programme. Recording could also be used to identify areas in which there may be a training need for a particular individual or group of employees.

For example if the employer of a group of workers in a call centre had trained those workers to use key words or phrases when dealing with customer queries on a particular topic, it would be legitimate to record a cross-section of calls and use them to identify which employees needed further training or as examples on a training programme for new staff to demonstrate the 'right' and 'wrong' way to handle a telephone call.

In the interests of national security

9.29 Interception may be carried out if its purpose is the interests of national security, but such interceptions can only be carried out by certain specified public officials.

To prevent or detect crime

9.30 It would be lawful for an employer to intercept employee communications for the purpose of detecting fraud, corruption or criminal activity amongst the workforce.

To investigate or detect unauthorised use of the system

9.31 Employers may decide to intercept or monitor their employees' communications in order to establish whether any unauthorised use of the system is taking place. For example, if a company policy stated that email was provided strictly for business use only, then monitoring could be carried out to establish whether any employees were breaching the policy by sending personal emails during working time.

It is important to note, however, that even though monitoring may be conducted for the purpose of detecting unauthorised personal use of the employer's computer system, this does not give the employer carte blanche to read through the content of an employee's personal emails. The supplementary guidance to Part 3 of the Employment Practices Code points out that an employer would have to be able to justify taking action to read a personal email by weighing up the intrusion into the employee's private life with the employer's need to know the content of the email. In many cases it will be enough for the employer to detect from an email's address and subject header that it is a personal email rather than a work-related communication. The employer could then set up a meeting with the employee in order to discuss the matter and establish whether unauthorised use of the system had in fact taken place.

If the company policy is that reasonable personal use of the telephone, email and the internet is permitted, monitoring could be carried out to establish whether, on the whole, employees are confining their personal use of the communications systems to within the bounds of reasonableness. Clearly it would be helpful in these circumstances if the employer provided specific examples of what they regarded as reasonable personal use.

To ensure the effective operation of the system

9.32 It is lawful for an employer to monitor their computer systems for the purpose of checking for potential viruses or other threats to the system, such as hacking.

In addition to the above purposes, monitoring of employee communications, *but not recording*, is permissible under the *LBP Regulations 2000* if it is done for one of the two purposes outlined at 9.33 and 9.34 below.

To determine whether received communications are relevant to the employer's business

9.33 This provision provides employers with authority to check employees' voicemail and email inboxes whilst they are absent from work (for

177

example if they are on holiday or absent on account of sickness) if the purpose of so doing is to identify business communications that need to be dealt with. It is important to note that if interception is done for this purpose, only monitoring is authorised, and not recording of the data monitored. If, therefore, the employer wishes to make records of the incoming messages that have been intercepted, they would need to obtain the employee's consent to such recording. It will be equally important to ensure that employees have been properly informed that communications addressed to them will be opened in their absence.

One further restriction under this heading is that only communications that are received during the employee's absence can be monitored, and not any pre-existing incoming emails, nor previous outgoing emails that are still in the computer system. Monitoring of these outgoing emails would only be permissible if the purpose of such monitoring was compatible with one of the other purposes contained in the *LBP Regulations 2000,* or unless the employee had expressly consented.

The phrase 'relevant to the business' is further defined in the *LBP Regulations 2000, Reg 2(b)* as:

'(i) a communication:

(aa) by means of which a transaction is entered into in the course of that business; or

(bb) which otherwise relates to that business; or

(ii) a communication which otherwise takes place in the course of the carrying on of that business.'

It is apparent therefore that any telephone calls or email messages that are personal or private in nature and unrelated to the employer's business will fall outside the scope of the Regulations. This is consistent with the advice given in Part 3 of the Employment Practices Code which is that emails that are clearly personal or private should not be intercepted, even where the employer has imposed a complete ban on personal use of email and the internet. Employers should not therefore be tempted in normal circumstances to open or read any of their employees' incoming or outgoing email messages that are obviously personal.

There may (arguably) be limited exceptions to this principle if, for example, there is evidence to suggest that the employee has been engaging in criminal activity or other malpractice, for example where it is reasonably suspected that the employee has:

• transmitted confidential information by email to an outsider without authorisation;

- forwarded pornographic material as an email attachment to a colleague or outsider; or

- made a defamatory statement about an individual or another organisation in an email.

Provided there were proper grounds (and not, for example, just a vague, whimsical suspicion based on a purely personal view) to believe that an employee's personal telephone messages or email communications were 'relevant to the business' in this way, then interception of those personal messages could potentially be justified. This is in contrast with monitoring of communications that are obviously private and unrelated to the business, which would not conform with the provisions of the *LBP Regulations 2000* and which would risk being in breach of the employee's right to privacy under the *HRA 1998*.

To identify calls being made to anonymous counselling or support helplines

9.34 This category includes the monitoring of calls to confidential or welfare helplines in order to protect or support helpline staff.

The employer must be acting for one of the above specified purposes in order for monitoring and/or recording to be lawful. The *LBP Regulations 2000, regulation 2(b)* states that the interception must be 'solely for the purpose of monitoring or (where appropriate), keeping a record of communications relevant to the [business].' Thus employers are not permitted to use these purposes as a shield for monitoring that is in reality for a different purpose. Monitoring for any other purpose, for example out of curiosity, will be unlawful.

When monitoring employees' communications might constitute an unacceptable invasion of privacy

9.35 Monitoring employees' private mail, telephone calls or email communications where there was no legitimate business need to do so would in all likelihood be in breach not only of the *LBP Regulations 2000* (unless the employee had given their consent to the monitoring) but also of the *HRA 1998*. *Article 8* of the *HRA 1998* (see 9.38 below) is the right to respect for private and family life, home and correspondence and any kind of unnecessary, unjustified or over-intrusive monitoring would be likely to be in breach of this provision.

The starting point for examining whether monitoring is lawful is to understand that any form of monitoring in the workplace will constitute an intrusion into employees' privacy. Monitoring may also undermine employment relationships and damage the mutual trust and confidence that plays a key role in employment. One general principle is that employers should seek to settle on the least intrusive method of monitoring that will meet their legitimate business objectives.

Part 3 of the Employment Practices Code in general requires employers to recognise employee interests and provide real justification for any intrusive monitoring practices (see 9.10 above).

The implications of the Human Rights Act 1998

9.36 The *Human Rights Act 1998* (*HRA 1998*) gives private individuals the right to take legal action against a public authority if they believe that one of their rights, as defined in the Act, has been infringed by that authority. This means that employees of public authorities can take a direct claim against their employer in a court or tribunal (as appropriate) if the employer infringes any of their rights under the *HRA 1998*.

Although the *HRA 1998* does not confer any similar benefit on private sector employees, it contains a separate provision which obliges courts and tribunals (as public authorities themselves) to interpret legislation, including employment law, in such a way as is compatible with the rights contained in the European Convention on Human Rights (and by extension the *HRA 1998*). Thus private sector employers are protected, albeit indirectly.

Although the *HRA 1998* confers rights on all citizens, it is possible in law for an individual to agree to waive their rights under the Act. For example, an employee who signs a document signifying their consent to email monitoring conducted by their employer is volunteering to waive their right to privacy in relation to their email correspondence.

The principle of proportionality

9.37 The European Convention on Human Rights contains a standard known as the principle of proportionality. This principle requires a balance to be struck between the rights of individuals as defined in the *HRA 1998* and the general interests of the community at large. In *Soering v United Kingdom* [1989] 11 EHRR 439, the European Court of Human Rights described the principle of proportionality as 'the search for a fair balance between the demands of the general interest of the community and the requirements of protection of the individual's fundamental rights'.

This means that the rights contained in the Convention and in the *HRA 1998* are not absolute rights that can be insisted upon irrespective of everyone and everything else. An individual's rights stand to be balanced proportionally against the interests of the community, ie the rights of others (including the rights of the employer and the rights of the individual's colleagues). This means that individuals' rights can be limited or restricted by their employer provided the employer can show that there is proper justification for such limitations. If, therefore, an employer applies a policy or procedure that is likely to infringe employees' rights to privacy under *Article 8*, this may be justifiable provided the policy or procedure is:

- designed to achieve a legitimate business aim;

- likely to achieve that aim in practice; and

- proportionate to the achievement of that aim.

This demonstrates the importance for the employer of:

- setting out clearly what the aim(s) of any employee monitoring would be;

- examining closely whether the means chosen to carry out the monitoring were likely in practice to assist the achievement of the aim(s); and

- ensuring that any monitoring carried out was appropriate, necessary and not excessive in relation to the achievement of the aim(s).

Article 8 – the right to privacy

9.38 *Article 8* of the *HRA 1998*, the right to respect for private and family life, home and correspondence, impacts upon a number of issues in the workplace including:

- CCTV surveillance of employees at work (see 9.45 below);

- searching of employees and their personal property (see 9.48 below);

- medical examinations and questionnaires (see CHAPTER 7);

- drugs screening programmes (see CHAPTER 7); and

- monitoring of employees' communications. 'Communications' in this context would include employees' telephone calls, voicemail, letters, memos, faxes, email correspondence, internet use and use of pagers, company mobile phones, laptops, palmtops and blackberries.

The principle of proportionality contained in the Convention (see 9.37 above) will, however, in most cases permit activities such as those listed above provided the employer can show that the monitoring they carry out is designed to achieve a legitimate business aim and is proportionate (ie appropriate, necessary and not excessive) in relation to that aim.

However, there will of course be the need to ensure that the data obtained from such activities is handled correctly and in accordance with the *DPA 1998*.

It was established by the European Court of Human Rights in *Halford v United Kingdom* [1997] IRLR 471, that employees at work do in fact have a right to privacy. The *Halford* case concerned a complaint brought by a senior police officer about the interception of her telephone calls at work without her knowledge or consent. The Court held that, where an employee has a reasonable expectation of privacy and is unaware that their communications are liable to be intercepted by their employer, it will be unlawful for the employer to carry out interceptions. This case also suggests, however, that the right to privacy can be asserted only where the employee reasonably expects their communications to remain private. If, therefore, an employee has been properly informed that their communications are to be monitored, or has given their consent to monitoring, then an expectation of privacy cannot be argued.

The most important matter for the employer to address before deciding whether to carry out activities which would amount to a breach of the right to respect for privacy (such as monitoring of employee communications) is to ascertain the aim of the particular activity and whether any proposed monitoring is relevant and proportionate to the achievement of that aim.

Monitoring as an intrusion into employees' privacy

9.39 Part 3 of the Employment Practices Code emphasises that workplace monitoring will be an intrusion into employees' privacy and may thus undermine employment relationships and damage the mutual trust and confidence that plays a key role in employment. Employers should therefore seek to settle on the least intrusive method of monitoring that will meet their legitimate business objectives. There are also implications under the *HRA 1998* (see 9.40 below).

Another potential problem that the Code identifies is the risk that confidential, private or otherwise sensitive information may be seen by staff who carry out monitoring in circumstances where they do not need to know it, or have no right to know it. In general, the Code of Practice requires employers to recognise employee interests and provide real justification for any intrusive monitoring practices.

How to reconcile compliance with the Employment Practices Code with the privacy provisions of the HRA 1998

9.40 There are a number of measures an employer can take, and should take, to ensure compliance with the *DPA 1998* whilst at the same time ensuring respect for employees' right to privacy under the *HRA 1998*. The starting point would be to nominate a senior person within the organisation to be responsible for ensuring the organisation's policies, procedures and practices comply with the *DPA 1998*. Other courses of action would include:

- training all line managers and others whose jobs involve handling personal data obtained from monitoring in the operation of the *DPA 1998* and in particular ensuring they understand their responsibility to maintain confidentiality with respect to personal information;

- giving careful consideration to the question as to who in the organisation should carry out monitoring activities;

- keeping to a minimum the number of people who have access to personal information obtained through monitoring;

- requiring employees who have access to personal information in the course of their work to sign confidentiality and security clauses and ensuring these are clearly stated to be contractually binding;

- reviewing on a regular basis what personal information about employees exists within the organisation, how it is held and whether it is still necessary and appropriate for the employer to hold it;

- carrying out regular reviews of whether personal information is out of date and should be destroyed; and

- ensuring all employees are aware of the nature, extent and reasons for any monitoring.

Policies on monitoring employees' communications

9.41 Because of widespread access to email and the internet in today's hi-tech workplaces, and because of the wide range of potential legal liabilities that can be created for employers as a result of misuse of these facilities, it is essential for employers to devise and implement comprehensive policies, procedures, rules and guidance notes for employees who have access to email and the internet in the course of their work. Such policies would normally include a statement outlining the employer's approach to monitoring and a specific procedure explaining what type of monitoring the employer carried out and how it was carried out.

Clearly every employer's needs are different, and there is no one policy or set of rules that will be appropriate for all businesses. In some larger organisations, it may be desirable to have different sets of rules for different groups of employees, depending on the requirements of their jobs and the degree to which they need to use email or the internet in the course of their work. For example employees who, because of the nature of their jobs, have access to confidential information, or who have authority to enter into contracts with suppliers may need to be monitored more closely than those who perform routine work that is not in any way sensitive to the organisation.

In general, an employer may wish to consider introducing some or all of the following:

- a policy governing access to email and the internet, together with security and confidentiality measures that employees must adhere to;

- guidelines on the extent to which employees may use email and the internet for personal or private purposes (if at all);

- (where reasonable personal use is allowed) clear guidance on the extent and type of private use that is permitted;

- rules on how email should be used, the content of emails and email etiquette, for example the type of personal information that may, or may not, be included in emails;

- rules governing how the internet should be used, whether and to what extent surfing is permitted, together with a clear statement on any uses that are prohibited, for example the viewing or downloading of pornography;

- a statement advising employees of alternative methods of communication, for example sending a confidential communication to an occupational doctor by internal post rather than by email;

- a policy on monitoring that explains the purpose(s) for which the organisation conducts monitoring, the extent of the monitoring and the means used to monitor employee communications;

- the ways in which the policies on the use of the employer's communications system are enforced and the penalties that will be imposed on any employee who is found to be in breach of the employer's policy or rules.

The purpose and content of a policy on monitoring

9.42 Although the *LBP Regulations 2000* authorise the interception of employee communications in a wide range of circumstances relevant to the business, it is nevertheless important to have a clear policy in place regarding any monitoring that takes place in the organisation. It is also necessary to obtain employees' consent to any monitoring that does not fall within the ambit of the *LBP Regulations 2000* (see 9.19 above).

The Supplementary Guidance to the Employment Practices Code makes it very clear that 'it is a fundamental requirement of data protection law that workers are aware of ... monitoring'. The Guidance also suggests that one way to achieve this is to 'establish, document and communicate a policy on the use of electronic communications systems'. It goes on to state that it is not only the employer's policy that will be important, but the day-to-day practice in the organisation will also be relevant, in particular if the employer does not always impose the policy or any rules consistently.

A policy on monitoring should:

- explain what monitoring activities the employer carries out and the extent of those activities;

- explain the purposes for which monitoring is carried out;

- make it clear that employees' telephone calls, email messages and internet access cannot be regarded as private; and

- nominate a senior person within the organisation whom employees may approach if they have any questions or concerns about monitoring.

Checklist on monitoring

9.43 A checklist for employers considering introducing systems for monitoring employees' communications is as follows:

- Should monitoring be designed primarily to highlight access rates, as a spot check on possible problem areas, or to monitor actual content?

- How will the data obtained as a result of monitoring be held (ie location, format and content of the data)?

- Will it be necessary for individual employees' names to be identified in the records obtained as a result of monitoring (in which case the provisions of the *DPA 1998* will be engaged)?

- Should monitoring be restricted to workers about whom complaints have been made, or about whom there are reasonable grounds to suspect misconduct?

- Should monitoring be targeted only at employees who work in jobs which pose a particularly high risk to the employer?

- In the event of a problem being identified as a result of monitoring (for example if an employee is found to have accessed an inappropriate website), what will the appropriate procedure be and how will the records be handled?

- What action will be taken against an employee who, as a result of monitoring, is found to have been misusing email or internet access?

- Who within the organisation will have the overall responsibility for carrying out monitoring and for the data protection issues arising from monitoring?

- Who will be given the task of carrying out the monitoring and what type of training (including training in the *DPA 1998*) will be required?

- How will employees be informed about the monitoring carried out by the employer, and the extent and frequency of the monitoring?

- What steps will be taken to ensure that monitoring is carried out fairly and lawfully and only for the purposes defined in the employer's policy?

- What steps will be taken to ensure the confidentiality of the results of monitoring?

- How will the policy be kept under review in the light of the results of monitoring?

Video and audio monitoring

9.44 The collection and processing of video images and audio recordings relating to individuals falls under the *DPA 1998* in the same way as information about individuals held on files or on computer. It will rarely be appropriate, however, for an employer to deploy video (CCTV) or audio monitoring within their workplace. Being subjected to video monitoring whilst working would be particularly intrusive for employees and likely to make many feel uncomfortable and inhibited in their work. Such monitoring would also be hard to justify, except in specialised circumstances. By contrast, a policy of CCTV recording in corridors within a building that is open to the public or in a company car park might, for example, be justifiable for reasons related to security or safety.

Employers should not therefore, as a general rule, conduct video or audio monitoring of their staff in the course of their work, unless there are special reasons to do so. Such special reasons might involve work areas where highly valuable items were handled by employees in the course of their work, for example expensive jewellery, or where particular safety risks existed and there had been previous incidents of breaches of safety procedures. Employers should not, however, consider installing cameras or microphones in areas where workers would have a genuine and reasonable expectation of privacy, for example in private offices or toilets.

Any employer that considers that they have special reasons that might justify video or audio monitoring of their employees should, in the first instance, conduct an impact assessment (see 9.11 above). Part 3 of the Employment Practices Code and the accompanying Guidance suggest that, when conducting such an impact assessment, the employer should aim to:

- restrict video or audio monitoring, if it is required at all, to areas of special risk where possible;

- confine monitoring to areas where expectations of privacy are low, for example areas to which the public have access;

- only use continuous video or audio monitoring of particular individuals in rare circumstances where this is justified;

- consider how subject access requests would be dealt with, in particular bearing in mind the duty to remove any information that identifies a third party from video or audio recordings before allowing disclosure to the person requesting access.

The final point above is a reminder that any video or audio recording in which a person features would be regarded as personal data under the *DPA 1998*. Thus, any person caught on camera or tape would have the right to request access to the video or audio tape.

As with other types of monitoring, the employer must inform employees (and others who may, for example, be caught on camera) what monitoring is taking place, where it is taking place (ie where any cameras or microphones are located), why the employer considers it necessary to monitor in this way and what the cameras or tape recorders are intended to detect. In most circumstances, a prominent notice informing people that CCTV cameras are in operation, why they are being deployed and where they are located will suffice.

CCTV monitoring

9.45 The *DPA 1998* applies to CCTV used in the workplace (and elsewhere). A Code of Practice on CCTV, published in 2000 under the *DPA 1998*, deals with CCTV surveillance in public areas and aims to set out the measures that must be adopted by CCTV operators in order to ensure compliance with the *DPA 1998*. The Code also provides guidance as to good practice in this area. The Code does not, however, apply to the use of surveillance techniques by employers to monitor their employees, and is thus outside the scope of this book. The monitoring of employees via CCTV is instead, governed by Part 3 of the Employment Practices Code (see 9.10 above).

Shopkeepers and others who use CCTV for the surveillance of customers need to make sure that they do not use the images for any other purpose, for example using such CCTV images to check whether a member of staff was doing their job properly would not be permitted.

In-vehicle monitoring

9.46 The *DPA 1998* and Part 3 of the Employment Practices Code will extend to cover in-vehicle monitoring whenever the data obtained from monitoring can be linked to a particular individual, usually the driver of the vehicle. Except when in-vehicle monitoring is required by legislation (for example the installation of a tacograph in a lorry), the employer should conduct an impact assessment (see 9.11 above) before introducing any form of in-vehicle monitoring. The purpose of the impact assessment will be to determine whether the benefits that are likely to be obtained from this type of monitoring justify the intrusion into employees' privacy that will be caused, in particular by the constant tracking of the location of the vehicle.

With respect to in-vehicle monitoring, Part 3 of the Employment Practices Code and the accompanying Guidance recommends that employers should:

- formulate and apply a policy that states clearly whether employees may use company vehicles for private purposes, and if so, the extent to which private use is permitted and any conditions or restrictions attached to both business and private use;

- make sure employees have been fully informed of the type and extent of in-vehicle monitoring that will take place and how the information obtained from monitoring will be used;

- consider whether any necessary monitoring can be conducted in such a way as to prevent the gathering of information about permitted private use of the vehicle, for example by installing a 'privacy button' or other arrangement that enables the monitoring device to be switched off.

The employer should also make sure they have obtained express consent from employees prior to conducting any monitoring of the movements of company vehicles during periods when the vehicle may legitimately be used for private purposes.

In the unlikely event that an employer decided that it was appropriate and necessary to carry out monitoring in relation to employees' own vehicles (for example if private vehicles were, by agreement, to be used for business purposes), it would be necessary for the employee to have given their free consent to the installation and use of any monitoring device. Such a course of action should only be contemplated if monitoring is absolutely necessary for business reasons, for example, to establish the extent of business use in order to reimburse the employee the appropriate costs.

Third-party monitoring

9.47   Third-party monitoring means obtaining information about employees from third-party organisations such as credit reference agencies, the electoral roll or the Criminal Records Bureau (or Disclosure Scotland) for use within the business.

As with other types of monitoring, the employer should carry out an impact assessment (see 9.11 above) before deciding whether to undertake any third-party monitoring. This should be done in order that the employer can properly determine whether third-party monitoring is necessary and appropriate for the business, and what the precise objectives would be of such monitoring.

Part 3 of the Employment Practices Code and the accompanying Guidance suggest that employers should:

- inform their employees whether any third party source of information is used to carry out checks, the identity of the third-party source, and why the particular type of checking is believed to be necessary and appropriate with respect to the needs of the business;

- inform employees whenever a specific check is to be carried out, unless doing so would be likely to prejudice the prevention or detection of a crime or serious malpractice;

- refrain from monitoring an employee's personal financial circumstances unless there are firm grounds to believe that there would be a significant risk to the business if the employee concerned was experiencing financial difficulties, for example in some parts of the finance sector where there might be a higher than usual risk of fraud;

- ensure any agency used to provide information about employees is aware of the use to which the employer intends to put the information that is provided to them;

- avoid using a facility that has been set up to check on customers or potential customers to vet or check up on employees;

- retain only the minimum amount of information provided by third parties about employees, for example record only the fact that a check took place and the overall result and, unless there are compelling reasons to do otherwise, delete the information after no more than six months.

Employee searches

9.48   The question as to whether an employer should conduct random searches of employees, their personal property, their files or lockers and/or their vehicles should be subjected to the same scrutiny as the prospective monitoring of employee communications. Searching employees will be highly intrusive and will represent a breach of the right to respect for privacy enshrined in *Article 8* of the *HRA 1998* (see 9.38 above). There will therefore have to be strong justification for any policy to conduct searching. It follows that any employer who is considering introducing a random employee search programme should:

- identify the aim of the proposed search programme, for example the aim might be to protect an employer in the retail sector against employee theft;

- establish whether the proposed search programme is necessary for and relevant to the achievement of the stated aim; and

- examine whether the carrying out of personal searches, locker searches or even searches of employees' vehicles is proportionate to the aim (ie appropriate, necessary and not excessive in relation to the employer's need to protect their business interests).

It may, for example, be proportionate to carry out searches in relation to employees whose jobs take them into contact with valuable equipment or materials (such as storekeepers and shop assistants), but excessive to apply the policy of random searching to office-based staff if, because of the nature of their work, they have little or no opportunity to access company equipment or materials.

Conclusion

9.49 In terms of adhering to data protection legislation when monitoring employees, the key to staying within the law whilst at the same time ensuring fairness is to adhere to the data protection principles and aim to strike a reasonable balance between the needs of the business to operate efficiently and lawfully, and the rights of employees to enjoy privacy and to be treated with respect. The level and nature of any monitoring should be proportionate to the employer's stated business needs, or to any specific problem that has been identified, for example an inordinate amount of time being spent by an employee visiting non work-related internet sites. Employees' explicit consent should be obtained before any data about them is collected, stored or used in any way.

Chapter 10 Freedom of information

Introduction

10.1 The *Freedom of Information Act 2000* (*FOIA 2000*) and the *Freedom of Information (Scotland) Act 2002* were implemented at the beginning of 2005, when the general right to obtain access to recorded information held by public authorities came into force. The Acts were fully retrospective and apply to all existing information, not just information filed since the legislation came into force. Private companies that provide a service that is part of the function of a public authority are also covered.

For the purposes of *FOIA 2000* (see the 'Freedom of Information Factsheet' on the Information Commissioner's website: www.ico.gov.uk) 'public authorities' will include:

- central government and government departments;

- local authorities;

- hospitals, doctors' surgeries, dentists' practices, pharmacists and opticians;

- universities, colleges and state schools;

- police forces; and

- prison services.

The Information Commissioner is responsible for promoting observance of the requirements of *FOIA 2000*.

Overview of the Freedom of Information Act 2000

10.2 The main features of *FOIA 2000* are:

- to provide members of the public with a general right of access to recorded information held by public authorities, subject to certain conditions and exemptions;

- to place public authorities under a duty to provide reasons for any refusal to supply the information requested;

- to impose a duty on public authorities to provide reasonable advice and assistance to people who are approaching public authorities seeking information;

- to oblige every public authority to adopt and maintain a publication scheme, and to publish information in accordance with the scheme.

The main underlying aim of the freedom of information legislation is to encourage openness and transparency. *FOIA 2000* provides individuals (and therefore organisations) with the right to request, and receive, any information held by any public authority (subject to certain exemptions – see 10.9 below). The right is to receive information that is held at the time the request is received, ie if the information requested is held by that authority, the applicant is entitled to be given it. If the information requested is not held, then there is no duty on the authority to provide anything beyond a written response informing the applicant of that fact.

The right of access applies to all recorded information irrespective of who created or who owns the information (subject to the permitted exemptions – see 10.9 below). This means that information supplied to the public authority by a third party (for example a private company) would be caught (see 10.8 below).

FOIA 2000 does not cover the right for an individual to access information held by a public authority about themselves, as this matter is covered separately under the *Data Protection Act 1998* (*DPA 1998*).

FOIA 2000 places a duty on public authorities to adopt and maintain an 'Approved Publication Scheme' and publish information in accordance with the Scheme. Schemes must be approved by the Information Commissioner. The Commissioner may approve model schemes for groups of similar bodies, for example universities, and a public authority may then adopt such a model publication scheme. A publication scheme is a guide to the classes of information that the particular public authority publishes and the possible exemptions applicable to each class, ie it acts like an index. A publication scheme:

- indicates the location of the information and the format in which it is published;

- says whether individuals may obtain the information free of charge or on payment of a fee;

- must include statements of policy on: freedom of information and data protection; records management; procedures for dealing with requests, including an address to which applicants may direct request for information or assistance; and procedures for internal review in the event of a decision not to disclose.

Codes of Practice and Guidance

10.3   The Secretary of State for the Department of Constitutional Affairs (DCA) has issued two Codes of Practice (available at: www.dca.gov.uk). These are:

- a Code Of Practice on the discharge of public authorities' functions under *FOIA 2000*, issued under *section 45* of the Act, which sets out the practices which public authorities should follow when dealing with requests for information;

- a Code of Practice on the management of records, issued under *section 46* of *FOIA 2000*, which gives guidance on the practices that public authorities should adopt with regards to keeping, managing and destroying records.

The *section 45* Code of Practice states that its aims are to:

- facilitate the disclosure of information by setting out good administrative practice that it is desirable for public authorities to follow when handling requests for information including, where appropriate, the transfer of a request to a different authority;

- protect the interests of applicants by setting out standards for the provision of advice which public authorities should provide and to encourage the development of effective means of complaining about decisions taken under the Act;

- facilitate consideration by public authorities of the interests of third parties who may be affected by any decision to disclose information, by setting standards for consultation; and

- promote consideration by public authorities of the implications for freedom of information before agreeing to confidentiality provisions in contracts.

Codes of Practice are not legally binding, but a failure to comply with their provisions may mean that the public authority is failing in its duties.

The DCA has also produced a suite of guidance that provides advice for public authorities on compliance with *FOIA 2000,* available at: www.dca.gov.uk.

The Information Commissioner has also published a set of 'Awareness Guides' which provide detailed, best practice guidance to public authorities on how they should fulfil their functions under *FOIA 2000* (available at: www.ico.gov.uk). For example, there is a document that provides the Information Commissioner's Guidance on the Act, which in turn is divided into four categories:

- procedural guidance, dealing with the practical aspects of the Act;

- technical guidance designed to assist public authorities in dealing with requests for specific types of information;

- sector-specific guidance aimed specifically at different types of public authority; and

- exemptions guidance dealing with the permitted exemptions under the Act.

The provision of advice and assistance

10.4 Public authorities are required by *FOIA 2000* to provide advice and assistance to people who have made or who are thinking of making a request. This will help applicants understand their rights under the Act and identify the information they are seeking. The Information Commissioner's procedural guidance suggests that examples of what is reasonable for a public authority to do may include:

- advising a potential applicant of their rights under the Act;

- keeping an applicant advised of progress with regard to their request;

- assisting an applicant to focus their request (if it is unclear), perhaps by informing them of the types of information available within the requested category;

- advising an applicant if information is available elsewhere, and explaining how to access this (for example via the public authority's publication scheme).

The *section 45* Code of Practice (see 10.3 above) recommends that if an applicant, even after receiving appropriate advice and assistance, is unable properly to describe the information they are seeking in a way that has enabled the public authority to identify and locate it, the authority should:

- disclose any relevant non-exempt information that has been successfully identified; and

- explain to the applicant why they cannot take the request any further; and

- provide details of their complaints procedure and the applicant's rights under *FOIA 2000*.

The interface between data protection and freedom of information

10.5 The *FOIA 2000* gives rights to everyone and is concerned with the public's right to access information about the activities of organisations in the public sector. The *DPA 1998*, on the other hand, gives rights to individuals concerning information held about them personally and addresses the right to privacy. Access requests under the *DPA 1998* can only be for access to 'personal data', ie information held about oneself.

An important point to note about the *DPA 1998* is that it applies to all organisations that hold personal data, including private sector organisations, unlike *FOIA 2000* which applies only to public authorities.

Requests for information

10.6 Anyone has a right to ask any public authority for any information they hold, regardless of when the information was created or how long it has been held. Information is defined as 'information recorded in any form'.

The applicant can ask:

- for a copy of the information they seek; or

- for the chance to inspect the records; or

- to be provided with a summary of the information.

The public authority should try to provide the information in the form requested unless it is not reasonably practicable for them to do so. Certain information is exempt (see 10.9 below), but disclosure will be the norm rather than the exception.

If the person making the request already has reasonable access to the information they want, then that means should be used. For example, if the information the person is seeking is available through the public authority's publication scheme, the public authority can simply direct the person to the scheme.

If the public authority does not hold the information requested, but believes that it may be held by another public authority, they should either:

- inform the applicant of this fact, and provide them with the contact details for the other public authority; or

- consult the other public authority to check if they do hold the information and, if so, consider whether transferring the applicant's request to them would be appropriate.

A request for information under the Act could, in theory, be received anywhere in an organisation as the applicant may not know the name of the person who has been charged with responsibility for dealing with *FOIA* requests. It is therefore important for public authorities to:

- put procedures in place for taking decisions about whether to disclose information at appropriate senior levels;

- conduct awareness sessions for all staff whose role brings them into contact with the public to ensure they are familiar with the core requirements of the Act;

- provide more detailed training to a sufficient number of staff so that they are able to identify a request for information under the Act and provide appropriate advice and assistance to applicants and assist other members of staff as needed.

Conditions for requests to be valid

10.7 There are three conditions that must be met in order for a request for information under the Act to be valid: These are as follows:

(1) The request must be made in writing or in another recorded form. Requests sent by email or fax are acceptable, provided they are legible. Requests in other recorded forms, such as audio or video tape, will also count. It will be important to bear in mind that any letter, fax or email that asks for information (whomsoever it is addressed to) may fall within the ambit of *FOIA 2000* and thus carry the force of the law. Telephone enquires do not carry the force of law but the person dealing with the call should provide appropriate advice and assistance to the caller on how to make the request for information (see 10.4 above).

(2) The request must state the name and address of the applicant. This provides a contact point for the public authority in the event that it might require further information from the applicant to assist it to identify and locate the information requested.

(3) The applicant must adequately specify and describe the information they are requesting. There is, however, no prescribed format. If the applicant has not provided enough details for the public authority to be able to identify and locate the information requested, the authority is entitled to ask the applicant to provide further information for that purpose, and explain to the applicant why they are asking for more information.

Further points to note are that:

- there is no requirement to quote the Act when submitting a request;

- there is no requirement for the applicant to give a reason for requesting the information – and public authorities should not seek to determine the aims or motivation of applicants;

- requests may be made by foreign nationals anywhere in the world;

- requests made by minors are valid requests.

Information that identifies third parties

10.8 Sometimes the provision of information requested under *FOIA 2000* will involve disclosing information about third parties or information supplied by third parties, and thus be likely to affect the third party's interests. In these circumstances, the public authority should:

- take appropriate steps to make sure that third parties who supply information to the public authority or about whom the authority holds information are made aware of the public authority's duty to comply with *FOIA 2000,* and that information about them or supplied by them may therefore have to be disclosed (unless an exemption applies – see 10.9 below);

- give advance notice where possible to the third party whenever the public authority proposes to disclose information about them or which affects their interests, or if this is not possible then draw the disclosure to their attention afterwards;

- consider whether any explanatory information should be given to the applicant along with the information they have requested, for example a notice that the information provided is subject to copyright restrictions.

Permitted exemptions

10.9 There are 23 exemptions from access in *FOIA 2000*, some of which are 'absolute' (unconditional) and some 'qualified'. Where an exemption applies, the public authority should not disclose the data requested to a member of the public. If a public authority believes that the information is covered by a qualified exemption, they must apply the 'public interest test' (see 10.10 below).

Public authorities are not permitted to impose blanket exemptions from access to particular types of information. Instead each case where refusal is being considered will need to be reviewed on its own merits on a case-by-case basis at the time the request is made.

The 23 exemptions are:

- information that is accessible elsewhere (for example in the public authority's Publication Scheme);

- information intended for future publication where it is reasonable to withhold disclosure until it is published;

- information supplied by, or relating to, bodies dealing with security matters, eg the Secret Intelligence Service;

- information that might substantially prejudice national security;

- information that might substantially prejudice defence;

- information that would substantially prejudice international relations;

- information that would be likely to substantially prejudice relations between any administrations within the United Kingdom;

- information that could substantially prejudice the economic interests of any part of the UK;

- information about investigations by public authorities and proceedings arising out of such investigations;

- information about law enforcement, including information that would be likely to prejudice the prevention or detection of crime and information relating to relevant civil proceedings brought by public authorities;

- court records;

- information the disclosure of which would substantially prejudice a public authority's auditing functions;

- information that is subject to parliamentary privilege, ie where the exemption is required for the purpose of avoiding an infringement of the privileges of either House of Parliament;

- information held by a government department which relates to the formulation or development of government policy, ministerial communications, the provision of advice by any of the law officers or the operation of any ministerial private office;

- information that could substantially prejudice the effective conduct of public affairs;

- any communications with Her Majesty or other members of the royal family, and awards of honours;

- information which, if disclosed, might endanger the health or safety of any individual;

- information about the environment which, although exempt from disclosure under *FOIA 200,* may have to be disclosed under the *Environmental Information Regulations 2004 (SI 2004 No 3391);*

- personal information about an individual, which must not be disclosed to another person if the disclosure would infringe any of the data protection principles (individuals may, however, be entitled to access information about themselves under the *DPA 1998);*

- information provided in confidence (see 10.11 below);

- information subject to a legal professional privilege;

- information that constitutes a trade secret or whose disclosure would be likely to prejudice the commercial interests of any person or organisation (see 10.12 below);

- information whose disclosure would be prohibited by law or would constitute a contempt of court.

Many of the above would be unlikely to apply in the employment context. However two of the exemptions (commercially sensitive information and confidential information) are examined further below.

Public interest

10.10 'Public interest' is not defined in the Act, but guidance is contained in the Code of Practice. 'In the public interest' means something that would be of serious concern or benefit to the public, for example information about something that could be of danger to public health, or to the environment. It does not mean something that would be 'of interest' to someone.

Essentially, if the public interest in maintaining the exemption outweighs that in disclosing the information, the information need not be disclosed. There should, however, always be a clear and defensible rationale for any decision taken to withhold information on the basis of the public interest test.

Confidential information

10.11 Confidential information is defined as information obtained from another person where its disclosure to the public would constitute a breach of confidence actionable by that person or any other person.

When entering into contracts with private companies, public authorities may be asked to agree to contractual clauses that purport to restrict or prevent the disclosure of the information provided by the private company (for example the terms or value of the contract). Public authorities should exercise caution in this area as they may be required under *FOIA 2000* to disclose the information upon request. It is advisable therefore for public authorities to make it clear to third parties that disclosure can be restricted only as permitted by the Act, for example if the information is genuinely confidential. Public authorities should make any company supplying confidential or commercially sensitive information aware of the implications of the Act.

The *section 45* Code of Practice (see 10.3 above) recommends that public authorities should consider making express provision in any contract with a private company as to what information will be regarded as confidential (and therefore not liable to disclosure under *FOIA 2000*) and the reasons for categorising the information accordingly.

If a request is made which would involve disclosing confidential information that was supplied by a third party (for example a supplier) prior to the Act coming into force, the public authority should consult the third party involved to see whether the requested information is still to be regarded as confidential.

With respect to the possible disclosure of confidential information, the duty of confidence is not absolute. The courts recognise three broad circumstances in which confidential information can be disclosed:

- where the parties consent;
- where disclosure is required by law;
- where there is an overriding public interest.

Commercially sensitive information supplied by a third party

10.12 If disclosure would be likely to prejudice substantially the commercial interests of any person, the information need not be disclosed. Similarly, if the information in question can be classed as a 'trade secret', it need not be disclosed.

The public interest test will rarely justify the disclosure of a trade secret. However, adverse commercial impact may, on its own, often be insufficient to justify non-disclosure, for example where disclosure would be in the interests of public health, safety or the environment. In these circumstances, the benefits of disclosure would be likely to outweigh any financial loss or prejudice to the competitive position of the third party company.

Timescales

10.13 Public authorities generally have 20 working days in which to respond to a request. There is, however, a provision in the Act which allows the 20-day time limit to be extended where the authority is required to apply the public interest test, because one of the qualified exemptions applies (see 10.9 above). In that case, the public authority must inform the applicant (within 20 days of receiving their request) that they need more time to consider the matter and must give an estimate of the date by which they expect to make a decision on where the public interest lies. The authority must then respond fully 'within a reasonable time'.

As stated in 10.7 above, if the public authority is unable to locate the information requested because the applicant has not provided enough details, the authority can ask the applicant to provide further information to help them to identify and locate the information requested. In these circumstances, the public authority is not required to comply with the request until that further information is provided.

Fees

10.14 Individual public authorities are, within defined restrictions, allowed to charge a fee for responding to requests for information. What can be charged is governed by the *Freedom of Information and Data Protection (Appropriate Limit and Fees) Regulations 2004 (SI 2004 No 3244)*. Charging is not, however, compulsory.

If the public authority wishes to charge a fee, it must inform the applicant of this fact in writing and specify the fee to be charged. In this case, the 20 days for responding to requests will be put on hold until the fee is paid. If the fee is not paid within three months, the public authority will be entitled to assume that the applicant no longer wants the information. The authority must write to the applicant confirming this.

Fees may be charged only if the actual cost of providing the information exceeds £600 (for central government and Parliament), or £450 (for all other public authorities). This means in effect that the first £450 or £600 of costs must be borne entirely by the public authority (except for the costs of photocopying, printing and postage, which may be charged). In estimating the cost of complying with a request, the public authority must calculate the cost of staff time at a rate not exceeding £25 per hour per staff member.

Public authorities are not permitted to charge for:

- providing information in their Publication Scheme;
- any costs incurred in determining whether the information requested is actually held;
- any costs incurred deliberating about whether or not to provide the information;
- extra costs incurred in providing information in a special format for a disabled person.

If the cost of providing the requested information is likely to exceed the £450 or £600 limit (as appropriate), the authority may:

- refuse to comply with the request on the grounds that the cost of complying would exceed the defined limit; and
- provide the applicant with an indication of what, if any, information could be provided within the cost limit; or
- offer to comply with the request on payment of an appropriate fee; or

- decide to provide the requested information without charging.

No VAT is charged on fees.

Refusing a request

10.15 There are several circumstances in which the public authority may legitimately refuse to provide the information requested by a member of the public. In this case, the public authority must issue a 'refusal notice' which must also set out details of the applicant's rights of appeal, both internally within the public authority organisation and to the Information Commissioner (see 10.16–10.17 below).

A public authority need not comply with a request for information if:

- one of the exemptions applies (see 10.9 above), in which case the applicant should be informed in writing of the basis for the refusal, which exemption has been relied on and, where relevant, the arguments under the public interest test (see 10.10 above);

- the authority considers that the cost of complying with the Act would exceed the defined maximum amount (see 10.14 above);

- if the request is vexatious, or made repeatedly, ie if substantially similar requests are received from the same person, other than at reasonable intervals.

A request may be regarded as vexatious if the applicant:

- has unreasonably refused or failed to identify sufficiently clearly the information they require;

- has unreasonably refused or failed to accept documented evidence that the information is not held;

- has an obvious intention to disrupt the public authority's work rather than genuinely wishing to obtain information.

However, inconvenience, irritation or nuisance caused by the request does not qualify as vexatiousness.

Complaints

10.16 If an applicant for information under *FOIA 2000* has a complaint about the way in which their request was handled, they should, in the first instance, use the relevant public authority's complaints procedure (if there is one). This allows the public authority itself to review its conduct in relation to any aspect of the request. The *section 45* Code of Practice recommends that public authorities should have a procedure in place for dealing with complaints in relation to their handling of requests for information (although this is not a legal requirement).

Where a public authority receives a complaint, they must review their handling of the request and/or the decision taken and provide the complainant with a written response setting out their decision, the reasons for the decision and the procedures for further appeal. The handling of complaints must be conducted in a way that is fair and impartial, and by someone who was not involved in the original decision. Public authorities should (according to the *section 45* Code of Practice) set their own reasonable target times for dealing with complaints and publish these.

The Code of Practice recommends that:

- where the outcome of a complaint is a decision that the information requested should be disclosed (whether in whole or in part), the public authority should disclose the relevant information to the applicant as soon as possible;

- where the outcome is a finding that the public authority's procedures were not properly followed, the public authority should apologise to the applicant and take appropriate steps to prevent similar errors occurring in the future;

- where the outcome is that the public authority's original decision to withhold information is upheld, the public authority should inform the applicant of this fact and advise them of the right (if they wish) to apply to the Information Commissioner (providing the necessary contact details) for a decision on whether the request was dealt with in accordance with *FOIA 2000*.

Any refusal notice issued by a public authority in reliance on one of the permitted exemptions must include either details of the internal complaints procedure or else a statement that the public authority does not have one.

Powers of the Information Commissioner

10.17 Individuals can apply to the Information Commissioner's Office for a decision about whether a request has been dealt with according to the Act if, for example, they believe there has been excessive delay or if they wish to dispute the application of an exemption or a refusal to provide information made on public interest grounds. The Information Commissioner will investigate the complaint and both the applicant and the public authority will be informed (within four months) of the decision in a 'decision notice'. Where appropriate, the decision notice will instruct the public authority what steps it needs to take to comply with the Act. This may include the release of the information requested within a certain timescale. Alternatively, the Information Commissioner may confirm the decision made by the public authority.

If either the applicant or the public authority disagrees with the Information Commissioner's decision they have 28 days to appeal to the independent Information Tribunal (see 10.18 below).

The Information Commissioner also has the authority to issue a public authority with an 'enforcement notice' where the Commissioner considers that a public authority has failed to comply with one or more of the requirements of the Act. The enforcement notice will state:

- what steps the authority should take to comply with the Act; and

- within what timescale.

Although an enforcement notice is similar to a decision notice in some respects, the Information Commissioner does not need to receive a complaint from an applicant that a request has been incorrectly handled before taking this form of enforcement action. The public authority may appeal against such a notice.

Appeals

10.18 Either party may appeal against a decision notice (see 10.17 above). Appeals go to the Information Tribunal or, in Scotland, to the Scottish Court of Session.

The Information Tribunal (or the Court of Session) may:

- uphold the Information Commissioner's decision;

- amend the decision (for example change the time-frame for release of the information requested); or

- overturn the decision.

Non-compliance with the notice issued by the Information Tribunal or Court of Session is likely to constitute a contempt of court.

Chapter 11 Conclusion

Introduction

11.1 HR managers may believe data protection issues are impossibly complicated. Whilst it is true that very detailed guidance (such as the guidance provided in this book) needs to be considered and followed, in practice most of the rules amount to little more than commonsense. Employees who believe that their confidential personal information is properly protected will work better and stay longer with their employer than those who believe the business rides roughshod over their rights.

However the manager responsible for data protection matters within the organisation must not be complacent. Regular checks should take place in areas such as passwords. Often good systems are set up but then employees become sloppy in their habits. Examples include:

- Passwords written on post-it notes left on PCs so that all can use them, when the password protection was set up to ensure exactly that did not occur.

- New members of staff giving information to callers over the telephone without checking basic security details first.

- Waste paper or computers not disposed of carefully enough so that others can access and read confidential information contained on the paper or on the PC.

Data protection – the law

11.2 Twenty-five years after the UK first introduced data protection legislation, the job of those involved in this area remains difficult. Data protection is one of the few areas of legislation that has broad principles and less than clear rules. Almost certainly, no organisation can be one hundred percent compliant. Nevertheless, businesses do need to take positive steps to ensure that they properly protect all the data that they hold on employees and on customers and suppliers. Many examples of such positive steps are provided in this book.

A good starting point is to look at the Information Commission's Audit Manual and undertake an audit, as is also suggested in the Employment Practices Code published by the Information Commissioner. Employers should look very thoroughly at both the process of application for jobs and the records that are kept once an employee joins the organisation. Some key actions will be to ensure that proper consents from employees are obtained for the various activities that may be undertaken in relation to their data. Activities will range from handling sickness records to putting pictures of employees on the corporate website, from installing CCTV cameras to monitoring emails, internet access and telephone calls. As a general principle, if the employee knows a particular use will be made of their personal data, then the employer can proceed with it, but the maxim should always be: 'if in doubt, spell it out'. It might be assumed, for example, that every employee would know that their emails might be read whilst they are on holiday so the business can be properly managed in their absence, but this is an area where the Information Commissioner says an employee should always be notified that such surveillance might take place.

It will also be very important for employers to review regularly their data protection procedures. New rules come into force all the time so it can be very useful to send the data protection policy document, employment contract term and privacy notices posted on the corporate website to lawyers to check on an annual basis. In addition, some organisations will find it useful to run an annual training course on data protection for managers and other employees whose jobs entail handling personal data. This will help to ensure that they fully understand and are up to date with the law in this important area.

Managing data protection is about how the organisation sets up methods to protect personal data about workers. This covers allocating responsibility, establishing what personal data are processed, ensuring employment practices are compliant with the *DPA 1998* and checking whether the organisation needs to notify the Information Commissioner about any data held. These benchmarks appear in all parts of the Employment Practices Code as many of them will be relevant to every employer. How far they are applicable and what is needed to achieve them will, of course, vary from employer to employer and depend very much on the size and nature of the organisation and its activities.

Data protection compliance should be seen as an integral part of employment practice. It is important to develop a culture in which respect for private life, data protection, security and confidentiality of personal data are seen as the norm. The Information Commissioner's guidelines on Managing Data Protection should be uppermost in the minds of HR managers and are outlined at 11.3 below.

The benchmarks

11.3

1. Establish a person within the organisation responsible for ensuring that all employment practices and procedures comply with the *DPA*

1998 and for ensuring that they continue to do so. Put in place a mechanism for checking that procedures are followed in practice.

2. Ensure that business areas and individual line managers that process information about workers understand their own responsibility for data protection compliance and if necessary amend their working practices in the light of this.

3. Assess what personal data about workers are in existence and who is responsible for them.

4. Eliminate the collection of personal data that are irrelevant or excessive to the employment relationship. If sensitive data are collected ensure that a sensitive data condition is satisfied.

5. Ensure that workers are aware of the extent to which they can be criminally liable if they knowingly or recklessly disclose personal data outside their employer's policies and procedures. Make serious breaches of data protection rules a disciplinary offence.

6. Allocate responsibility for checking that the organisation has a valid notification in the register of data controllers that relates to the processing of personal data about workers, unless it is exempt from notification.

7. Consult Trade Unions or other workers' representatives, if any, or workers themselves over the development and implementation of employment practices and procedures that involve the processing of workers' data.

If these steps are taken, then most organisations should be able to achieve compliance with data protection legislation.

Data protection compliance should also be seen as part of wider legal compliance. Some other areas of law will overlap with it. Many employment policies are set up to ensure no sex, race, religious, sexual orientation, age or disability discrimination takes place. A regular review of policies is therefore necessary not only because of changes in data protection law, but also on account of changes in other areas of legislation.

There is a close overlap between data protection law and the law of confidentiality. Trade secrets, customer lists, business information and other valuable know-how must be protected and employees trained so they do not discuss confidential business matters with others, nor inadvertently disclose confidential information.

Those bodies within the state sector and thus caught by the *Freedom of Information Act* need to ensure their policies are compliant with that legislation too (see CHAPTER 10).

At its best, data protection legislation ensures employees are protected and respected, their rights to privacy treated seriously and both the employee and the employer gain. Where instead employers breach the legislation, staff turnover will be high, public damage will be done to a company's business reputation, and a criminal offence will occur with potential fines being imposed and the risk of expensive damages actions being started.

Notification

11.4 It is a legal requirement for data controllers to provide notification to the Information Commission on an annual basis (see CHAPTER 3). A fee is payable on first notification and on annual renewal of the notification. As a result of the notification, an entry is placed in the register of data controllers that the Commissioner maintains. This register is open for public inspection. The exceptions to notification are limited to some core business functions and some not-for-profit organisations. Data controllers who are exempt from notification may, however, notify voluntarily.

Because there can be only one entry in the register for each organisation, it is important to establish who in the organisation is responsible for data protection matters and specifically, for making the notification. Notification is a legal requirement and failure to notify when not exempt is a criminal offence. Equally, each legal entity in a group of companies must have its own register entry (unless it is exempt from notification). There cannot be 'group' notification covering a number of associated companies.

The HR department will inevitably process sensitive personal data so this will need to be included in the notification (unless the organisation is exempt). If the register entry is incomplete, it will need to be amended to include the processes of HR and the payroll function. Equally, they may have been treated as being exempt from notification, and if this is the case the register entry should contain a note about exempt processing.

Amendments can be made to the notified particulars whenever they are found to be incorrect or become out of date. No additional fee is due for amendments. It is a criminal offence to fail to keep the notification up to date.

Notification includes a statement about the organisation's security measures in respect of personal data. This statement is not, however, published as part of the public register. The employer can draw up the security statement by answering a series of questions that are available in the notification process. Answering 'no' to all the questions is permitted, but will not show that the data controller understands his or her responsibilities for data security under the *DPA 1998*. The result is likely to be that the Information Commissioner's office will query the notification. One further very important point to remember is that an exemption to notify is not an exemption from the requirements of the *DPA 1998*.

Employee records

11.5 The overall responsibility for ensuring that the processing of employee records complies with data protection legislation will usually fall to a senior HR director or manager. Nevertheless, line managers and staff alike will have to be aware of their responsibilities and duties under the Act if the employer is to achieve full compliance. It will be up to HR, however, to make sure that all staff, and in particular those whose jobs take them into contact with personal data held about employees, fully understand their responsibilities under the *DPA 1998* and that they receive full training in data protection matters.

The *DPA 1998* was introduced largely to promote openness and transparency of information held about individuals in filing systems, whether manual or computerised, and to provide a specific entitlement for individuals to gain access to any information held about them. The eight data protection principles contained in the *DPA 1998* underpin an employer's duties and obligations to process all personal data in a fair and proper way and ensure information is collected and retained about employees (and job applicants) only where it is necessary for the business. Employers are, irrespective of their size or business sector, required to determine the purposes for which they obtain and use personal information about their employees and ensure the information is not subsequently used for any incompatible purposes. Employers must also ensure personal information is held securely and not disclosed without authority. Other obligations include the duty to ensure that the information held about employees is accurate, is not excessive in relation to its purpose and is not retained for any longer than it is legitimately needed. All these issues will need to be managed and handled by HR.

The Act, and the accompanying Employment Practices Code, aim to encourage employers to strike a balance between their reasonable need to create, keep and use records about their staff and the rights of employees to respect for their private lives. The Code of Practice, although not legally binding, represents the Information Commissioner's recommendations as to how employers should fulfil their legal requirements under the *DPA 1998*. In the event of a legal challenge, a court or tribunal can take the Code into account, and any evidence that the employer has not complied with the recommendations contained in the Code are almost certain to operate to their detriment. Much of the Code is concerned with proportionality, ie whether a particular course of action carried out by the employer is appropriate and necessary for the achievement of a legitimate aim when balanced against the needs of the individual, including the right to privacy.

Awareness of data protection issues and the taking of the necessary steps to ensure compliance with the law come into play in a number of key HR activities, starting with recruitment and selection, which, inevitably, will represent one of HR's most important responsibilities.

In order to comply with the *DPA 1998* during the process of recruitment, employers should, for example, be upfront about disclosing their identity (ie not seek to conceal their identity from job applicants); use different application forms to ensure the information they collect about job applicants is restricted to that which is relevant to the job in question; ensure applicants' consent is obtained before conducting any checks, for example reference checks or checks on qualifications; and ensure the security of all job applications, including those sent in online. At the end of the recruitment exercise, employers should notify any applicants whose details they wish to retain on file, giving them the option to ask the employer not to retain them, and in general retain recruitment records for as short a period of time as necessary, based on stated business needs. Clearly it is advisable for HR to devise and implement a policy on the handling, retention and disposal of job applications, including unsolicited applications, so that every aspect of the *DPA 1998* can be fully complied with.

The creation and maintenance of employment records will form the foundation of effective people management, irrespective of the size of the business. If employment records are structured, well-organised and incorporate only information that is appropriate and relevant to the employer's needs, they will serve the employer well and aid compliance with the *DPA 1998*. HR should therefore devise and implement a clear and comprehensive policy on employment records, including, for example, a statement as to whether records should be held only by the HR department, or whether line managers may also hold certain types of records about their staff. It may be helpful also for the HR department to conduct an exercise to establish what personal information about employees exists within the organisation other than in the HR department, where it is held and who is responsible for it. Security of records, both manual and computerised, will be another important responsibility, often shared amongst the HR department, IT staff and line managers.

Other key points for HR in relation to employment records are to ensure all new staff are informed about what records are to be held about them; the source(s) of any information held about them; the purpose for which the records are to be held; how the information will be used; who it will be disclosed to; and what their rights are under the *DPA 1998*. Furthermore, it is a sound idea for all employers to devise a policy that will ensure the efficient handling of subject access requests.

With regard to the specific retention periods for different types of employment records, proper policy decisions should be made, for example the length of time that leavers' files and recruitment files will be retained. Once such policy decisions have been made, they should be consistently adhered to and HR should have in place a system to ensure the regular clearing out of records both from files held manually and from their computer systems. The decision as to how long to retain employment records should be based on business needs and should be made objectively. Records should not be maintained 'just in case' they might be needed at some future point in time.

Employers will need to pay particular heed to the provisions of the *DPA 1998* (and the provisions contained in *Article 8* of the *Human Rights Act 1998*, ie the right to respect for one's private life) when considering any form of monitoring within the workplace. Equal opportunities monitoring, for example, represents a valid and useful tool for identifying and tackling discrimination and promoting equal opportunities, but the investigation and record keeping associated with monitoring is controversial as some people may object to being asked questions about (for example) their ethnic origins or religion. Nevertheless, the collection of certain types of information may be required by law; for example, it may be necessary for an employer to collect and retain data about a disabled employee's condition and its effects if they are to be in a position to fulfil their duty under the *Disability Discrimination Act 1995* to make reasonable adjustments for that employee.

Other types of monitoring may prove to be even more controversial, for example drugs and alcohol screening, or where an employer operates a policy of monitoring employees' use of email and/or the internet. Such monitoring will need to comply with legislation such as the *Human Rights Act 1998* and (in the case of email/internet monitoring) the *Lawful Business Practice Regulations 2000*, as well as with the *DPA 1998*, assuming a record is kept of what was monitored. Nevertheless, it can be argued that some monitoring is a necessity for many employers in order to protect their interests, together with those of their staff and their clients.

The main aim in designing monitoring should be to strike a reasonable balance between the need to monitor as judged against employees' rights in contract, including the mutual duty of trust and confidence, and the right to privacy under the *Human Rights Act 1998*. HR should plan to carry out an impact assessment before any decision is made on a policy of monitoring. The impact assessment should be used to establish whether there is justification for monitoring in a general sense and also to review whether or not monitoring in specific circumstances would be justifiable.

One key issue in relation to the prospective monitoring of employee communications will be to decide whether monitoring will be designed primarily to highlight internet access rates (as a spot check on possible problem areas) or to monitor actual content. Essentially, monitoring should be carried out only where it is necessary and relevant to the business, and where the legitimate business needs of the employer outweigh the inevitable intrusion into employees' private lives. Even where it has been established that a degree of monitoring is a business necessity, steps should be taken to minimise the level of intrusion into employees' private lives whenever possible.

Health records

11.6 Any records that relate to an employee's physical or mental health held in the context of employment will have to be treated with particular care and respect, taking into account the duty of confidentiality owed by employers to their employees. Data about an individual's physical or mental health is one of the categories of information that is regarded as 'sensitive data' under the *DPA 1998* and must be treated accordingly, taking into account the need to minimise any intrusion into employees' privacy.

In general, employers should consider carefully whether they actually need to collect and hold information about their employees' health and if so, what level of detail is genuinely necessary to ensure their business interests. Some basic data will be held simply to support the payment of Statutory Sick Pay, whilst specific information about employees' health or illness may be needed to administer occupational health schemes. More detailed information may be gathered as a result of medical examination and testing.

It is strongly advisable to separate information about employees' health from information about absence. For example, it will only be necessary, when deciding whether to pay sick pay, to record the fact that the employee is unfit for work under his or her contract; the nature of the sickness will be immaterial to the question of whether to make payment. It may also be useful to segregate the health data that is held into two types: that which the employee may volunteer (such as the information needed to join the employer's occupational pension scheme) and that which the employer gathers compulsorily.

The best way to establish whether there is justification for holding information about employees' health is to conduct an impact assessment, in particular in relation to information that is gathered compulsorily from employees. This task would normally fall to the HR department to organise and coordinate. An impact assessment should aim to identify the purpose(s) for which health information is to be collected and held, and the potential health-related risks to the organisation. Any adverse impact on employees that is likely to be caused by the collection and use of health information should also be established, as well as any possible alternatives (ie alternative ways of addressing the risks other than the collection of health information about employees). Ultimately, the impact assessment will enable the employer to decide whether or not collecting and holding health information is justified, taking into account the obligations that arise out of the collection and holding of such information. If justification exists, the employer should still aim to keep the collection and retention of health information to a minimum.

The employer should of course, use properly qualified staff to undertake the collection of health information. For medical examinations and testing, it will be essential to use health professionals who will adhere to their own codes of conduct and ethical standards. Furthermore, suitably qualified health professionals should be employed to interpret health information and judge an employee's fitness for his or her particular job.

It is also advisable to limit access to health records so that only health professionals with a need to know are able to access personal health information. Employers should avoid holding health data in employees' general personal files or in the payroll department and should instead use a separate system whenever possible. Health data should be retained only for as long as it is needed. For example, once samples for testing have been examined and the results established, the samples themselves should be destroyed. If the testing was implemented in order to enforce an organisational rule on drug and alcohol abstinence, negative results can and should be destroyed. If an audit trail is needed, the employer should use the test administration rather than the medical data gathered as evidence that the testing was in fact carried out.

Similarly, local managers should not be allowed to gather any health data on their own initiative and should be clearly instructed to pass on any health data which they obtain quickly and confidentially to the organisation's HR department.

To ensure the competent handling of health, sickness and attendance data, the employer should draw up procedures for the handling of health records, ranging from sickness certificates through to information obtained as a result of medical examinations. The procedure should include details of where and how particular records are to be held, eg in payroll, HR or within the occupational health department.

Employees will of course expect all their health data to be treated with the same high levels of privacy and confidentiality as they receive from their own general practitioner.

Index

Data subjects
 notification, 3.5
Disability
 information about
  sensitive data, 5.18
Disability discrimination, 7.15
 collection and retention of data,
  8.14
 disability, meaning, 8.14
 equal opportunities monitoring,
  and, 8.14
 'long term' meaning, 7.15
 reasonable adjustments, 7.15, 8.14
Dismissal
 drugs and alcohol testing, and, 7.22
Drugs and alcohol testing, 7.20–7.22
 consent of employees, 7.20
 dismissal following positive result,
  7.22
 legitimate grounds for, 7.20
 policy formation, 7.20
 purpose, 7.20
 safety, and, 7.20
 selecting employees for, 7.21
 steps to be taken, 7.20
Employee monitoring, 9.1–9.49
 adverse impact, 9.13
 alternatives to, 9.17
 assessing appropriate type, 9.16
 audio, 9.44
 business needs, and, 9.49
 CCTV, 9.45
 checklist, 9.43
 covert, 9.8
 dealing with information obtained
  from, 9.9
 different forms, 9.7
 Employment Practices Code, 9.10
 impact assessments, 9.11
  benefits, 9.12
 implications, 9.18
 importance of, 9.1
 interceptions, 9.16
 inter-relationship between Data
  Protection Rules and Lawful
  Business Practice
 Regulations 200, 9.19–9.34
 in vehicle, 9.46
 justification for, 9.15
 Lawful Business Practice
  Regulations 2000, 9.19–9.34
   compliance with regulatory and
    self-regulatory practices or
    procedures, 9.27

Employee monitoring—*contd*
 Lawful Business Practice
  Regulations 2000—*contd*
   data protection principles, and,
    9.20–9.24
   ensuring effective operation of
    system, 9.32
   establishing existence of facts
    relevant to business, 9.26
   ensuring that personal data is
    adequate, relevant and not
    excessive, 9.24
   identifying calls to anonymous
    counselling or support
    helpline, 9.34
   investigating or detecting unau-
    thorised use of system, 9.31
   monitoring of employees'
    communications, 9.25
   national security, 9.29
   obtaining and processing per-
    sonal data for specified and
    lawful purposes, 9.23
   obtaining consent, 9.22
   prevention or detection of crime,
    9.30
   processing personal data fairly
    and lawfully, 9.21
   'relevant to the business', 9.33
   relevance of received
    communications, 9.33
   standards when using employer's
    systems of communication,
    9.28
 meaning, 9.2
 minimising intrusion into employees' privacy, 9.14
 policies on monitoring
  communications, 9.41–9.43
  content, 9.42
  matters to be considered, 9.41
  purpose, 9.42
 potential benefits, 9.5
 privacy of employees, and, 9.18
 protected records, 9.3
 purpose, 9.4
 responsibility for, 9.6
 searches, 9.48
 specific checks, 9.16
 spot-checks, 9.16
 third-party, 9.47